MW01257739

SELF-ESTEEM
WITHOUT
SELFISHNESS

INCREASING OUR CAPACITY FOR LOVE

Originally published as *Amor y autoestima* © Ediciones Rialp, S.A. Madrid, 2010.

Translated from the Spanish by Devra Torres

This translation published by Scepter Publishers, Inc., © 2013
P.O. Box 1391
New Rochelle, NY 10802
www.scepterpublishers.org

The total or partial reproduction of this book is not permitted, nor is its transmission by any form or by any means either electronic, mechanic, photocopy or other methods without the prior written permission of the publisher.

Scripture texts from the New and Old Testaments are taken from The Holy Bible Revised Standard Catholic Edition © 1965 and 1966 by the Division of Christian Education of the National Council of the Churches of Christ in the United States. All rights reserved. All copyrighted material is used by permission of the copyright owner. No part of it may be reproduced without permission in writing from the copyright owner.

Cover and text design by Rose Design

ISBN: 978-1-59417-189-5

Printed in the United States of America

15 14   2 3 4

SELF-ESTEEM
WITHOUT
SELFISHNESS

INCREASING OUR CAPACITY FOR LOVE

Michel Esparza

 Scepter

Contents

Introduction

This book is primarily addressed to ordinary Christians who, despite their defects, struggle day by day to increase the depth of their love. It may also be useful for those unfamiliar with the Christian life. Who wouldn't want to learn the key to a stable inner peace, self-esteem without delusions, and a marked growth in their capacity to love? More and more people find themselves immersed in a world so stressful that they must resort to medication to help them cope. More and more are convinced that the time has come to seek a new solution. I think the best advertisement for the Christian life is to show the irreplaceable help it offers for increasing our ability to love. In short, I intend to demonstrate that the awareness of Christ's love is able to purify all other loves and fulfill the heart's deepest longings, thus securing—even in this life—the greatest happiness.

As I write these lines, I'm thinking especially of those men and women who are easily discouraged when they become aware of their failures, whether in the Christian life or in any other sphere of their existence. They are often good-hearted people with a tendency to perfectionism—and therefore perpetually dissatisfied, or at least not altogether content. They live uneasily with themselves, because they don't know how to be patient with their own mistakes. Even their successes can never seem to outweigh the negative opinion they have of themselves. They turn almost everything into an oppressive obligation and are left with little margin for enjoying whatever they're doing. They know how to suffer, but happiness is something to be postponed until certain future conditions are met. This inner disquiet hampers their relationships with those around them.

My goal is to help these people see that as Christians, their imperfections and failures, far from being reasons for discouragement, can paradoxically be transformed into grounds for gratitude. Truly knowing we are children of God is what enables us to live at peace—with ourselves and others.

When I share with people that the Christian life, rightly understood, can help them to accept their own imperfections, offering the best solution to their troubles, they often ask me to recommend a book that explores these ideas in greater depth. Unfortunately,, the abundant bibliography with which I'm familiar ranges from simple self-help manuals to profound texts that treat this question of self-acceptance only peripherally (the autobiography of St. Thérèse of Lisieux is a good example). This is one factor that led me to write and publish this book.

The human and the divine are interwoven along the road to a successful life: human maturity—which is really nothing but mental health and common sense—grows together with Christian maturity, which brings about a robust supernatural vision. Since supernatural maturity beautifully complements human maturity, this book follows the same script. In the first part, I address questions of an anthropological nature, which are accessible even to readers unfamiliar with the Christian faith. As I share the ideal development of affectivity and personality, I show the importance of cultivating a positive attitude towards oneself without straying from the truth. To designate this positive and realistic attitude, I introduce the term "humble self-esteem." I demonstrate how the opposite attitude, which is "pride," generates all sorts of conflict and compromises the quality of one's love. The second part of the book centers on Christian spirituality as a means of solving the problems that come from pride. We'll consider together those aspects of God's love that, by revealing our dignity, are most helpful for strengthening a healthy attitude towards ourselves.

This is not a self-help manual of prefabricated solutions for the insecure. My focus is more on *principles* applicable to all rather than *recipes* useful to some. Immutable truths reveal the end to be attained; they inspire us to find our own paths to the goal but do not direct our every step. One needs both firm principles and flexibility in their application to each person's concrete situation. When opening doors, one should keep in mind that each lock has its own key. Thus, as I suggest solutions to universal problems, some readers may recognize themselves; others will doubt that my words have anything to do with them. The underlying theme, though, will (to varying degrees) be useful to everyone, since no one is exempt from the difficulties born of pride. We all need to learn to accept the truth about ourselves. As C.S. Lewis has written:

> There is one vice of which no man in the world is free; which everyone in the world loathes when he sees it in someone else; and of which hardly any people, except Christians, ever imagine that they are guilty themselves. I have heard people admit that they are bad-tempered, or that they cannot keep their heads about girls or drink, or even that they are cowards. I do not think I have ever

heard anyone who was not a Christian accuse himself of
this vice.[1]

In every human being there is some wretchedness and
some grandeur. We all must learn to reconcile our personal
imperfections with the greatness of being children of God.
Christian humility, rightly understood, unites our wretchedness and our dignity. According to St. Josemaría Escrivá,
humility is "the virtue which helps us to recognize, at one and
the same time, both our wretchedness and our greatness."[2] At
first glance, reconciling these two extremes appears to be a
contradiction. I hope the reader finds in these pages an aid to
integrating that seeming opposition: to understand and live
the joy of feeling oneself to be simultaneously wretched and
immensely loved by God. I think that "to recognize, at one
and the same time, both our wretchedness and our greatness"
is the key to Christian humility.

Humility is one of the most difficult and essential virtues. Developing and strengthening a good relationship with
oneself is no easy task. But it is worth the trouble—not only
our inner peace but also the happiness of all our relationships
depends on it. Indeed, experience shows that *the quality of
one's relationship with oneself determines the quality of one's relationships with others.* As Aristotle said long ago, in order to be
a good friend to others, one must be a good friend to oneself.

To some, it might seem strange to speak of the central-
ity of self-love, as if this were a kind of egotism—something
clearly incompatible with the idea of the virtue of humility.
However, a proper love of self and an egotistical *amor propio*

---

1. C.S. Lewis, *Mere Christianity* (Westwood, NJ: Barbour and Company, 1952),
p. 102.

2. J. Escrivá, *Friends of God* (London: Scepter, 1981), no. 94, p. 137.

are inversely proportionate to each other. As we shall see, an egotistical person loves himself not too much, but *wrongly* or *not enough*. The humble person, by contrast, is patient and understanding with his own limitations, which leads him to treat others' shortcomings with similar forbearance. There is a close relationship between *being loved, loving oneself,* and *loving others.* In the first place, we need to be loved in order to love ourselves. Knowing that someone loves us makes us aware of our dignity. There is also a connection between the attitude we have toward ourselves and the quality of our love for others. In order to live at peace with those around us, we must first be at peace with ourselves. Nothing separates us so much from our neighbor as dissatisfaction with ourselves. We know from experience that the most ardent faultfinders are usually those who have developed an attitude of hostility towards themselves. It makes sense that a disturbed attitude towards oneself would hamper a good understanding of others. First of all, someone preoccupied by his own worries is unlikely to pay much attention to those of others. Secondly, someone displeased with himself tends to overreact with others. It isn't easy to put up with someone else when one isn't able to put up with oneself.

Nothing helps us value ourselves so much as the experience of unconditional love. If we have never encountered this, how can we love ourselves, knowing that we have so many defects? Complexes—of inferiority or superiority—wear down our inner peace and our relationships with others, and they only disappear to the degree that we love someone who loves us just as we are. But can any of us receive a love so enduring and unconditional from any fellow creature? Isn't God the only one capable of this kind of love for us? True, human love is more tangible, but it is of a "quality" far inferior to divine love. A mother's love hints at a better understanding of divine love, but no mother can be at our side all our life, nor always gracious toward every single one of our defects. The love of our parents or good friends gives us enough security to take our first steps in life, but experience shows that this love, in the long run, turns out to be insufficient.

In fact, we can see that our ability to love in a fully stable and unconditional manner depends ultimately on the discovery of the love of God. In order to love ourselves just as we are, without any deception, we need to discover the advantages of our own frailty before a merciful Lover.

A theoretical grasp of God's love is insufficient. We need something palpable, a living experience. And for this, a special grace is needed. Of course, no spiritual progress is possible without the aid of divine grace. Great life transformations are the fruit of a close collaboration between God's grace and a person's freedom. But when it comes to living out the humble pride of a child of God, one needs a profound and radical change of mentality. There is a progressive and mysterious interior transformation, through the warmth of grace, sometimes in the midst of particularly painful life circumstances, which makes the soul especially receptive to the divine movements within it.

Like everything else in life, this progress in the gradual abandonment of our own esteem into God's hands implies *desire*, *knowledge*, and *ability*: good will, formation, and capacity. Divine aid facilitates all three: it strengthens our will, enlightens our understanding, and heals our powerlessness. But God, who respects our freedom implicitly, always desires our collaboration—our efforts to improve and learn to be humble.

St. Josemaría once said that books are never finished; they are only interrupted.[3] Without the inestimable help of my brother, Rafa, and my friend, Jos Collin, it would have been very difficult ever to "interrupt" these pages. I am grateful for their constructive criticism, the strongest proof of their affection, and I hope these intuitions that I have committed to writing will facilitate the irreplaceable action of God's grace in the souls of my readers.

LOGROÑO, NOVEMBER 28, 2008

---

3. V. Messori, *Hipótesis sobre María* (Madrid: Libros libres, 2007), p. 411.

Part One

PRIDE AND ITS DIFFICULTIES

1.

In Search of Dignity

In this first part, we will look at the principal problems associated with an unhealthy relationship with oneself. For various reasons, this subject is very popular today, although the topic is not new. Very ancient texts have addressed both pride and charity towards oneself, and these speak to the same reality—albeit with their own terminology and from their own perspective. Nonetheless, the growing influence of the field of psychology has added a new dimension to the importance of getting along well with oneself, and thus the term "self-esteem" (having a positive attitude toward oneself) was coined. A persistent, magic halo seems to hover above this term. Step into any bookstore and you'll observe the proliferation of self-help and self-improvement books, each insisting upon the importance of discovering, accepting, and developing one's own identity. The common thread for many of them is the emphasis on self-esteem's role in the balanced development of the personality.

SELF-ESTEEM AND HUMILITY

I don't doubt that encouraging self-esteem per se is positive—unless one proposes to do so by any means and at any cost.

The questionable effectiveness of some of the methods these books promote provides good ground for caution. A friend of mine, who is very much drawn to this sort of self-help approach, once took me to his house and showed me an exceedingly complex (and expensive) stereo system designed to transmit subliminal, barely perceptible messages throughout the night. He slept with earphones on, using a series of tapes with suggestive phrases such as "You're terrific"; "You're so valuable"; "You are unique"; and "Even if others don't appreciate you, you're great." Predictably, this vibrant fantasy never did produce the desired effect.

Some of the methods promoted by certain self-help books are wrongly oriented and can prove harmful when introduced into our education system. Thus, we find teachers who, out of their fear of creating guilt feelings, try to convince their pupils that they are devoid of defects. These teachers thus seek to inculcate self-esteem in their students *at the expense of the truth about themselves.* It's all very well to prevent and combat inferiority complexes, but not at the cost of respect for reality by making children and young people believe themselves to be better than they are. The truth will come out, sooner or later, and the deception, once unmasked, will inevitably lead to deeper frustration.

In the United States, for decades now self-esteem has been encouraged among young people with a simplistic psychology whose chief maxim is "Above all, always feel good about yourself! Never forget that, whatever you may do, you're a fabulous person!" But the outcome can be as pernicious as the one shown in a 1989 study that compared the mathematical abilities of students across eight countries. The American students finished last, the Koreans first. The researchers then investigated the self-esteem of these same students, inquiring into their opinion of their own aptitude for math. The result was the inverse of the objective reality: The Americans came in first, the Koreans last.[1]

Speaking of self-esteem is all very well as long as it involves accepting the *whole* truth about oneself—both positive and negative, thus avoiding the complexes of inferiority *and* superiority. These extremes, by defect or by excess, are both reflections of the same damaging and frustrated pride. It is just as harmful pedagogically to encourage a self-deception that refuses to acknowledge shortcomings as it is to focus on the flaws of those already prone to exaggerating them. It's not a question of "thinking that everything we do is wonderful by the mere fact that it is we who do it, but of refusing to treat ourselves too harshly. We are who we are and, in the end, we ought to be our own best friend. We won't shut our eyes to everything within us that can or ought to improve, but we are not to force this improvement by means of punishment or disdain . . . Let us acknowledge the good that is in us without stridency or wild fanaticism, but if there are grounds for pride, then, for goodness' sake, let's be proud."[2]

Humility and self-esteem are inherently related yet distinct concepts. Whereas humility is a moral virtue, self-esteem has its origin in psychology. The latter refers to a positive feeling about oneself. Humility, though, is far more than a mood: it implies a profound acceptance of the inner truth, good or bad. And it goes far beyond this, as we shall see, in that it also establishes the awareness of dignity.

Ultimately, one of our deepest problems lies in the way we hide and reject our imperfections instead of learning how to

---

1. Cf. P. C. Vitz, *The Problem with Self-Esteem*, *www.catholiceducation.org*.
2. P. Gómez Borrero, *La Alegría* (Barcelona: Martínez Roca, 2000), pp. 12–13.

accept them. Ideally, we should acknowledge them and then peacefully seek out the means of addressing them. This truthful and realistic attitude constitutes the essence of the virtue of humility. The vice opposed to it is called pride or arrogance. "Arrogance" always has a negative connotation, but "pride" is not necessarily pejorative. In a positive sense, I can be proud of my country or my family. Unhealthy pride, on the other hand, indicates a flawed relationship with myself that leads me to despise those who don't share my sympathies. Some languages have a term that designates solely the positive sense of pride (*fierté* in French; *fierezza* in Italian). From now on in this book, I will use the term "pride" in a negative sense. It will serve to refer generically to a poor relationship with oneself. The term "arrogance" includes a distinctive feature: an air of superiority.

Nuance is important; *generalization* is dangerous. When it comes to humility, distinctions like the ones we've been making about self-esteem are necessary. Humility aids us in cultivating a healthy relationship with ourselves and peacefully accepting the reality of our wretchedness. Pride, by contrast, distances us from the truth, preventing us from acknowledging our limitations. When we fail to recognize our flaws, we have two basic alternatives. One, by defect, consists of simply imagining that we have none. This *classic arrogance* involves a naïve optimism doomed to clash with reality. The other attitude, by excess, leads us to exaggerate our weaknesses. Here we have an *inverted arrogance*, or *false modesty*, which entails a radical pessimism and can nourish a self-pity that is poisonous to our mental health. Someone who seeks to exaggerate his virtues is proud, but so is someone who exaggerates his defects. The humble person, by contrast, is ruled by the truth. He knows that false modesty is just as contrary to humility as classic arrogance is. He avoids feelings of superiority *or* inferiority. He understands that he shouldn't take himself too seriously, but he doesn't undervalue himself either.

Each of these nuances has important pedagogical consequences. While the teacher seeks to prevent classic arrogance, he shouldn't defend inverted arrogance. If he disregards this, he runs the risk of inculcating a negative self-image at all costs. He thus falls into the error opposite to the one committed by "self-esteem education." On the one hand, self-esteem suggests a positive self-image—but it can distance us from the truth. On the other hand, humility leads us to the truth but can instill in us an unhealthy self-image.

Thus, superficially grasped, self-esteem and humility might seem mutually exclusive. For those with a mistaken understanding of humility, self-esteem will inevitably suggest a prideful attitude. And those with a false understanding of self-esteem will deem humility harmful to mental health. If we delve more deeply, though, we will soon realize that authentic humility is the best antidote to an inferiority complex, and that self-esteem does not necessarily conceal any form of egotism. I still recall the disconcerted expression on a friend's face when I told him bluntly that he had problems with humility because he didn't love himself. He asked me what I was talking about; it was clear that he couldn't imagine the two concepts connected. I had to clarify that humility meant self-forgetfulness, whereas he was continually preoccupied with himself because his imperfections made him feel contemptible.

In fact, *self-esteem and humility are mutual correctives.* Humility reminds us that self-esteem ought to be bound to truth. And self-esteem counteracts the negative image we may have of humility when we're not focusing correctly. Given that humility needs to be complemented by a sense of dignity, I use the expression "humble self-esteem" to refer to the virtue opposed to pride. The ideal attitude towards ourselves leads us to humbly acknowledge the truth about our own imperfection but also includes a profound sense of our own dignity.

A Grave and Ancient Problem

Gauging the dimensions of pride, in all its permutations, is key to unraveling many of the difficulties we manage to create for ourselves—difficulties which, when they emerge from our inner world, negatively affect our relations with others. C.S. Lewis hits the nail on the head when he says:

> [Pride is the] chief cause of misery in every nation and every family since the world began. Other vices may sometimes bring people together: you may find good fellowship and jokes and friendliness among drunken people or unchaste people. But pride always means enmity—it is enmity.[3]

The consequences of this are both patent and grave. Hearing of the horrible killings among African tribes, a child asked, "Why do they hate each other so much?" To which an old man replied, "Perhaps they hate each other because, being alike, they insist on wanting to be different."[4]

What is at the root of all this wretchedness? Where does pride come from? To respond, we need to go back, far back, both in humanity's history and in each individual's lifetime. We all enter the world with the problem of egotism; it nestles in the human heart. We know this from experience. Even

---

3. Lewis, *Mere Christianity*, p. 104.
4. A. Vásquez-Figueroa, *Africa llora* (Barcelona: Plaza y Lllanes, 1994), pp. 204–205.

children, long before attaining the age of reason, give proof of it. They are envious; they tend to crave attention; they want to be the center of the universe. Thus we have the paradoxical syndrome of the "dethroned prince" apparent in an older sibling upon the joyful welcoming of a new baby.

An expert pediatrician once told me that even babies just a few months old can behave with hysteria. He recounted the case of a six-month-old child who suffered episodes of apnea. Once the baby observed the understandably worried reaction of his mother, he resorted to this trick frequently. In this pretense, the baby found the most effective way of capturing his mother's attention. "I'll cure him," the pediatrician told her, "if you just leave him with me in the hospital for a week." Indeed, in a few days the child was completely cured. When the mother asked the doctor what treatment he had used, he told her he had simply paid no attention each time the child seemed unable to breathe.

The sickness of pride and its effects are within us from the beginning. How can we explain this? Are we designed improperly, or did something happen to damage our nature? Resolving this mystery surpasses our intellect's ability. According to Catholic doctrine, this question is linked to a grave sin of pride *at the dawn of human history*. Bl. John Paul II affirms that original sin is "truly the key for interpreting reality."[5]

---

5. John Paul II, *Crossing the Threshold of Hope* (New York: Knopf, 1994), p. 228. Let us briefly recall the doctrine of original sin. We arrive in this world with a "fallen nature." God created us to be happy, loving as he loves. However, our nature has deteriorated, due to the stain left by the first (original) sin of history, and continues to deteriorate due to our own personal sins. The Book of Genesis recounts how man was made in the image and likeness of God (see Gen 1:26–27) but, because of a sin of pride, was separated from him. Instead of allowing himself to be exalted by his Creator, he preferred to grasp independence and seek excellence on

PRIDE IS COMPETITIVE AND BLINDING

We would do well to identify the mechanisms that pride uses to ensnare us. Each of us is born with a tiny, insatiable tyrant within. Whoever is ruled by pride, even if he achieves every one of his objectives, will never feel wholly satisfied. He will never manage to fill the void; that would require an absolute esteem, one that this world cannot give.

Besides being insatiable, pride is essentially competitive. If pride is what motivates us, even someone whose merits are equal to our own is enough to make us feel restless and drab. Because of its insatiability and competitiveness, pride engenders envy and dissatisfaction. If not corrected in time, it gives rise to all kinds of tensions. In today's society, we see frequently that "it's a question not of being competent, but competitive. It's not enough to be rich: I must be richer than my brother-in-law. What's important is not to write a good book but to write one that sells more copies than the last one. I've got prestige, but that's still not enough."[6]

I once knew someone who always felt dissatisfied professionally, even though he had earned six degrees. Whenever he

---

his own. As a creature, man is necessarily a limited being, but he is "the only creature that God has loved for his own sake (Vatican Council 2, *Gaudium et spes*, no. 24) and has been given an immortal soul capable of receiving divine gifts. Sadly, our first parents rejected this divine offer. Since this "original split," man has gone about madly in search of his lost dignity. That which gave rise to the first historical sin, a pure arrogance, has been set up within our nature. And all subsequent sins have done nothing but exacerbate the situation. One might say that the wounds of sin have become anchored in our genes, our habits, our neurons . . .

As theology explains, by reason alone we would never have discovered the existence of original sin, although once revealed, its reasonableness is clear (cf. Thomas Aquinas, *Summa contra gentiles*, book 4, chapter 52; and J. H. Newman, *Apologia pro vita sua*, Brand, Bussom, 1948, pp. 312–314).

6. A. Llano, *La Vida Lograda* (Barcelona: Ariel, 2002), p. 86.

got a good job, he'd leave it, aspiring to a different one that he coveted still more. It's a shame to see people who focus greedily on work alone, neglecting their loved ones. It's worth reminding them that their present professional success is only the past of their future, which will arrive, sooner or later, with their retirement and a depressing balance sheet, humanly speaking, apart from the area of work. Even if they have built up an economic emporium and are surrounded by admirers, a moment will come when they feel, or are made to feel, superfluous. At first, perhaps, they justify themselves by claiming they want the money to raise their family. But sooner or later it will be clear that their prime motivator was pride.

Pride is not only competitive: it is blinding. It acts as a funhouse mirror. And if the power of self-criticism is absent, each step forward becomes tortuous. It is like a virus introduced into the most obscure corner of the soul, impossible to treat, since the patient is unaware of the infection. For example, cancer cells, though foreign to the body, are not recognized as such by the immune system. Analogously, pride comes in a more twisted form than other vices, veiled in various disguises. Its *modus operandi* consists of hiding to conceal its repulsive countenance. Thus it manages to contaminate even the noblest pursuits. It slips in, disguised as a passion for defending the truth, as wisdom, as self-consistency, as an impassioned struggle for justice. . . . The more self-knowledge one attains, the more infected areas are exposed.

Pride introduces an element of falsity into one's perception of both self and others. At once blinding and competitive, it leads us to view others as potential rivals, threats to our own excellence. We thus project upon them our own urge to feel superior. Since the thief believes everyone to be like himself, others appear as rivals or, worse, as domineering tyrants who threaten to overpower his own independence. This self-projection mechanism is particularly perilous in relation to God and helps us to understand "the obscure but real fact of original sin."[7]

The arrogant think of themselves as superior; they seek to play the role of king, if only within the "kingdom" of their own wretchedness. They grow competitive and distrustful, even of their Creator. They fall into a sort of megalomania, supposing themselves God's equals. Thus—although with less lucidity—they fall into the same temptation that, according to Genesis, preceded the first sin.

Projecting one's own arrogance onto God amounts to a dramatic inversion of reality. Love is God's sole motive for creating human beings, but we are distrustful of him. God desires, above all, to be a most loving father, but his creatures turn him into a kind of despot, the jealous guardian of his own supremacy. According to Bl. John Paul II, at the heart of atheism is the reaction of someone fleeing a false image of God that he himself has invented, having exchanged the father-son relation that God always wanted for a master-slave one.

> The Lord appears jealous of His power over the world and over man; and consequently, man feels goaded to do battle against God. No differently than in any epoch of history, the enslaved man is driven to take sides against the master who keeps him enslaved.[8]

Rebellion against God ends up harming man. Having discarded the deepest source of his dignity, it stands to reason that he ceases to be respected as a person. "Man begins by

7. John Paul II, *Crossing the Threshold of Hope*, p. 227.
8. John Paul II, *Crossing the Threshold of Hope*, p. 228.

devaluing God," observes Pilar Urbano, "and ends up reduced to a digital statistic. . . . To diminish God is, ineluctably, to shrink man down as well . . . upon rounding the corner of ignorance of God, one finds oneself in the blind alley of ignorance of man."[9] Recent history painfully confirms that the denial of God, whether theoretical or practical, entails contempt for human dignity. We see this not only in the genocides of the twentieth century but also in the ongoing attacks on incipient human life. As Bl. John Paul II noted in 2000, humankind "has achieved an extraordinary capacity to intervene in the very origins of life; he can also use these capacities for the good, within the framework of the moral law, or else succumb to the myopic pride of a science that accepts no limits, arriving even at trampling on the respect due to every human being. Today, as never before, humanity is at a crossroads."[10] Current ethical relativism comes in the guise of altruism, but beneath this "myopic pride," one can discern a rebellion against the only Lord of life and death.

MATURITY: THE WORK OF A LIFETIME

Cultivating humble self-esteem is the work of a lifetime. No one is exempt from the task of maturation. This involves many factors that include genetics, education, and the use we make of our freedom. We are all born with weaknesses that may eventually be aggravated by adverse life events or personal mistakes. We must, therefore, take a brief detour into

---

9. P. Urbano, *La madre del ajusticiado* (Barcelona: Belacqva, 2005), p. 38.

10. John Paul II, homily of October 8, 2000 ("Act of Entrustment to Mary"). On the impact of this urgent call of John Paul II, see J. Herranz, *En las afueras de Jericó* (Madrid: Rialp, 2007), pp. 373–375.

the field of pedagogy, since the most harmful conditions are the ones found during the period of greatest vulnerability: childhood and adolescence.

When toddlers take their first steps, they begin to realize their own neediness but are incapable of reasoning about it; they are unaware of the inalienable dignity that is due them as persons. They tend to call attention to themselves in a spiral that only parents can arrest, teaching them that they are precious in God's eyes. If the parents fail in this, they will quite possibly end up as helpless witnesses to the abundant insecurity and drama that will develop as time goes by. Adults are often unaware of the wounds they inflict on their children. At times, this deep mark becomes apparent only as the years pass—as, for example, in the always-disconcerting confrontation among siblings over an inheritance. The explanation often lies in a long and remote history of injured pride.

Educating a child is always a tricky and worrisome challenge. It is a far-from-intuitive job that has as much science as art about it. Many parents unconsciously transmit their own defects to their children. A healthy pedagogy combines the appeal to good behavior with an acceptance and love of one's own limitations. Parents need to show children that they are loved unconditionally—not for what they have, know, or manage to do but because they're loved as they are. Emotional blackmail is as common as it is dangerous. It is a mistake to teach children that the affection they receive depends on their success in adjusting themselves to the tastes of the adults around them, instead of encouraging them to do good freely, out of love, and not simply to win approval.

Educating someone in the desire for perfection can nourish a false, unreal "I" unless this goal runs parallel with the importance of accepting oneself as one is. Otherwise, the stage is set for anxiety and tension. If the subject in question doesn't accept himself as he is, he will attempt to satisfy the impossible demands imposed by his false, idealized "I." He may try to imitate some ideal character, while repressing his real, legitimate personality.

If one doesn't learn this essential lesson within the family circle, it will be much more difficult to assimilate it later, outside the home. This becomes clear upon making the leap from a toddler to a school-age child. What a child encounters in this new arena is often the closest thing to the law of the jungle: Whoever is noisiest and most intrepid is the most powerful. From this point onward, depending on personality, some will accentuate their arrogance, affirming themselves by humiliating other children. Others will become victims of a growing shyness (which functions as a defense mechanism), seeking self-esteem through academic success. These introverted ones grow isolated, with few friends; the arrogant, by contrast, become the bosses and, for fear of losing their "prestige," feel duty-bound to behave more and more aggressively. In both cases the trigger is the same: a lack of acceptance.

THREE LIFE STAGES

The path toward recognizing one's own value is mapped out for us by those people whom we value in a particular way. These are our "significant others"[11] who, when they judge us, wield a decisive power over our self-image. We see this clearly in the three stages of life: childhood, adolescence, and maturity.

---

11. The expression "significant other" originates with G. H. Mead (see H. Arts *Een Kluizenaar in New York*, Anberes: De Nederlandse Boekhandel, 1986, p. 23).

In childhood, our significant others tend to be our parents (especially fathers for sons and mothers for daughters). When children reach the age of reason, they become aware of their own neediness and turn to their parents' opinion to ascertain their worth. Later, around puberty, they begin a difficult but necessary period: the search for identity independent of parental opinion. In both cases, between about six and twelve years of age, one's receptivity to parents and teachers is at its height. This is the best time to plant a seed.

The second phase is adolescence, which stretches, generally speaking, from ages thirteen to twenty. The distinguishing mark here is the gradual loss of the child's receptivity, reflected in the formation of judgments that don't coincide with those of parents and teachers. The parents' task now grows more complicated. This is the time to help children construct a life plan, but in a way that respects their freedom—accompanying them closely but fostering a legitimate independence. The relationship of authority should gradually give way to one of friendship and confidence. At the other extreme, an overly protective and possessive parental attitude will in all probability impede a child's maturation.

In adolescence one's new significant others are one's friends. The adolescent realizes that he must determine his own self-worth, but he doesn't usually achieve this, continuing instead to weigh his worth against the judgment of those he most admires. If he learns to overcome human respect and defend his own opinions, and if he surrounds himself with good friends—who value him for who he is and not what he can offer them—all will be well. If not, he won't dare reveal himself as he is and will tend to fall in with an unscrupulous crowd. The consequences of the adolescent's mimicry can be dismal. If he moves in circles lacking in values, he'll imitate whatever behavior is in fashion to avoid feeling out of place. Sexual promiscuity, delinquency, or drugs are a few of the countless possible consequences.

Especially sad are those promiscuous girls who demean themselves, offering their charms to the first comer. The real reason behind their behavior is not so much sexual attraction but vanity. To "like themselves," they need to feel that they can attract boys and then brag about their "conquests" to their "emancipated friends."

Between the ages of twenty and twenty-five, at the height of youth, one ought to have adopted a personal, stable outlook. In adolescence, out of self-affirmation, children often adopt a posture contrary to that of their parents. The definitive "launch," though, comes when they learn how to dialogue, adopting convictions of their own but remaining open to the enriching effect of others' views. They enjoy self-confidence, but not obstinacy, for they are also capable of healthy self-doubt. They follow their own life plans freely, but they have become reasonable and willing to accept advice. They have now become, in fact, sufficiently mature to realize that life is a never-ending learning process.

The third and definitive stage of awareness of one's dignity should commence with adulthood but, sadly, many alleged adults are still ruled by the same self-affirmation mechanisms observed in childhood and adolescence. If they were truly mature, instead of allowing others to dictate their worth, they would discern it for themselves. Instead, they spend their whole lives playing at a sort of comedy, with the added difficulty that their urge to count as "good enough" is more complicated than that of the child.

Many adults persist in a dependence on the opinions of others. In their quest to make a good impression, they are liable to sacrifice anything. And, in the end, being ruled by "human respect" is not worth the effort, since people tend to judge us according to superficial criteria: whether we're easy to get along with, the kind of car we drive, and so on. Only those who truly love us take more notice of *who* we are than *what* we have, know, or can do for them.

Human respect can seriously compromise the authenticity of our relationships with others. In a simple novel, we find this keen observation:

> As soon as a few of us get together, we don't dare to be who we really are, because we're afraid of being different from the way we think everyone else is, and everyone else is afraid to be different from the way they think we are. So we all pretend to be less pious, less virtuous, and less honorable than we really are. . . . It's what I call the new hypocrisy. . . . In the old days, people pretended to be better than they were, but now they pretend to be worse. In the old days a man said he went to church on Sundays even if he didn't, but now he says he plays golf, and would be very distressed if his men friends find out that he really went to church. In other words, hypocrisy, which used to be what a French writer called "the tribute that vice pays to virtue," is now "the tribute that virtue pays to vice."[12]

Some are insecure and go around begging for appreciation: they can only see themselves through others' eyes. Others seem to have overcome human respect: they are independent and no longer affected by "what people will say," but they achieve this through self-sufficiency. They don't care what people think of

---

12. Bruce Marshall, *The World, the Flesh, and Father Smith* (Boston: Houghton Mifflin Co., 1945).

them because of their disregard for others. Possibly, at its root, this is a defense mechanism. Some of those who boast of their independence are, consciously or not, retreating into themselves for fear of rejection. In a Susanna Tamaro novel, the heroine, who has always boasted about being a free spirit, admits at the end of her life that, deep down, fear of not being appreciated has been her guide. In a farewell letter to her daughter, she writes:

> I can tell you that it's fear that has determined my life: what I called audacity was really panic. Fear that things might not be the way I had decided they would, fear to cross a boundary that was not in the mind, but the heart; fear of loving and not being loved in return. In the end, this is really man's only terror, and it is the reason we fall into mediocrity. Love is like a bridge suspended over the void . . . out of fear, we complicate simple things, so as to follow the ghosts of our mind; we turn a straight road into a labyrinth we don't know how to escape. It's so hard to accept the rigor of simplicity, the humility of surrender.[13]

It is well known that the Chinese feel very much ashamed to make a mistake in public. They call it "losing face." Confucius said that a man needs his face as a tree needs its bark. How can we avoid this slavery to human respect? This fear of "losing face" vanishes before those who truly love us—thus the importance of knowing the One before whom it is impossible to "lose face." We tend to see our reflection in others as in a mirror, and there is no more flattering mirror than the eyes of someone in love. This is why we ought to learn to see ourselves through God's eyes. Only someone who takes God as his or her "significant other" can go through life free

13. S. Tamaro, *Listen to My Voice* (London: Harvill Secker, 2008), p. 235.

of every kind of complex. Children depend on their parents' esteem. Adolescents depend on the approval of their friends. But those who have reached true maturity are the most independent of all, because they see themselves as God does.

THE LIFELONG SEARCH FOR LOVE

The love we receive plays a decisive role in our progress towards maturity. Pride sinks its roots into the hunger for esteem with which we are all born. And what best satisfies this hunger is love. Nothing lends us so much dignity as feeling—or knowing—that we are loved. If we feel someone's love, we think, "This means there's something in me that attracts this person, something worth loving." Other aspects of life—success at work or skill at sports—have their influence, too, but these sources of self-esteem are less wholesome, and also less effective, than love bestowed and received. If achievements that are noble in principle are not oriented towards love, they'll end up at the service of pride and bring nothing but dissatisfaction in the end. Professional and social "glory" is gratifying but transient. In times of success, we take less notice of an inner emptiness, but eventually there comes a resurgence of the hunger for love we all bear within us. If we're honest with ourselves, we'll agree with Henri Nouwen, who, describing his inner state before his conversion, acknowledges, "I was still the slave of my heart, hungering for love, in search of false paths to gain my own self-esteem."[14]

Problems born of pride don't suddenly vanish, of course, even when we decide to seek happiness solely through love, leaving behind the false promise of transient professional and social successes. Something more is still lacking. Only God's

---

14. Henri Nouwen, *The Return of the Prodigal Son* (New York: Doubleday, 1994).

love can really fulfill our profoundest longings. For a permanent resolution to the problem of pride, we need to discover that the only sure source of self-esteem lies in God's unconditional love. The love we get from relatives and friends doesn't ultimately reconcile us with ourselves. This human love, apart from its conditional aspect, often brings disappointment and the search for temporary solutions. Let us look at how this works throughout the different stages of life.

Infancy is fascinating in this regard. The infant has a palpable yet unconscious experience of the closest thing to unconditional love: a mother's love. However, this "state of grace," perceived at such an early age, does not last. It's one of life's laws. During adolescence, we realize that our parents' love is not as unconditional as it had appeared: we understand for the first time that the road to independence is healthful, and we begin to acknowledge our own worth for ourselves. As an initial solution, if we don't attempt to fill the emptiness through academic successes, we hope to find this unconditional love in friendship. In the long run, though, this proves to be no definitive solution, since even best friends have their limitations.

Carmen Martín Gaite portrays in one of her novels the reunion of two friends from adolescence, thirty years later. One of them writes afterward in a letter:

> We've grown. To grow means to separate from others, of course: to acknowledge the distance and accept it. The enthusiasm of those juvenile encounters with people who awakened our interest was founded on our taking for granted a continual permeability throughout our lives and their own, our problems and theirs. A union seemed possible. It's true that there are still moments when this illusion of permeability arises, but they are extraordinary

and fleeting: you can't expect them to last. When I was a young girl—and the same was true for you—I was sure that the people who loved me would never ignore me, that my life was indispensable to their own. What I really wanted, though, was for them never to stop needing me. But it doesn't work like that. Later you see that it doesn't, and that it's better for nobody to need you very much.[15]

Love between a man and a woman has great power to satisfy the hunger for esteem. Thus, with one's first success at love, quite a few problems of insecurity seem to disappear. It often happens that those who had wild swings of self-esteem in adolescence are suddenly cured when they fall in love and their love is returned. Falling in love produces a sort of enchantment that makes a person think he or she has found an unconditional, divine love that has nothing to do with petty calculations and getting along with each other in day-to-day life. A person in love lives ecstatically, enraptured, thinking continually of the beloved. Plato noted long ago that this sort of love is a reflection of divinity. The things lovers write to each other could come from the mouth of God himself, with the difference that, for God, love is not blind. On the other hand, the mirage of falling in love makes the defects of the beloved scarcely visible: it persuades us that no one is better than him or her. It's not surprising that people in love say to each other, "I adore you"— something that, strictly speaking, corresponds only to God. As Bécquer expresses it in one of his poems:

What the savage does, when with clumsy hand
Of a log he makes a god, at whim,

---

15. C. Martín Gaite, *Nubosidad variable* (Barcelona: Anagrama, 1992).

And then bows down before his own handiwork,
You and I do, too.[16]

Only the love of God can wholly fulfill us, but the love of our fellow creatures helps us to establish our self-esteem. At the end of the day, every human love is a reflection of divine love, and that reflection intensifies in the measure that the "quality" of the human love increases. The relationship between quality of love and humble self-esteem is a reciprocal one. On the one hand, the more love we receive—and the truer the love, the more this is so—the more our self-esteem increases; on the other hand, as we shall see throughout the next chapter, an attitude of humble self-esteem is essential to increasing the depth of the love we give.

Human love is a good starting point, though it is meant to be completed by divine love. One psychiatrist came to this conclusion after being involved in a traffic accident and experiencing palpably the affection of his family and friends. He said to himself:

You've finally understood that if you've never had the experience of being loved, it's very difficult to love. But this experience isn't enough. This horizontal love between children and parents, husband and wife, isn't sufficient. The vertical experience—the person's experience of God—is needed as well. For one thing, human love by itself is insufficient. It is only illuminated and acquires its sense and its full meaning in divine love.[17]

16. G. A. Bécquer, *Rimas y leyendas* (Madrid: Elección Editorial, 1983), p. 37.
17. A. Polaino-Lorente, *Una vida robada a la muerte* (Barcelona: Planeta, 1997), p. 203.

2.

Making Progress in Love

Cultivating humble self-esteem is one of the best ways to combat the problems of pride, and it's indispensable for improving all our relationships. So far, we've explored the many difficulties that stem from pride. In this chapter, with a more positive slant, we'll focus on the relation between humble self-esteem and the quality of love.

Nothing offers us more happiness than true, genuine love. Certainly, material well-being contributes to our happiness, but our greatest joy arises from giving and receiving love. This was the conclusion of a professor from the University of Rotterdam who made an inventory of more than 6,000 writings on this topic. He found that those with lower incomes exhibited a higher level of satisfaction.[1] On the other hand, the more perfect the quality of the love, the more happiness is procured from it. In a deep love, the essential element is not the enjoyment but the sharing, and the greater the communion, the more enjoyment. The egotist seeks possession and remains permanently dissatisfied. By contrast, those who,

---

1. See F. Javaloy, *La eterna búsqueda de la felicidad*, supplement to *La Vanguardia*, January 6, 1996.

instead of seeking their own advantage, act for the good of the beloved experience unexpected joy each time they succeed. And if this deep love is mutual, a surprising "spiral" ensues, giving rise to unsuspected heights of bliss.

THE NECESSITY OF TRUST

The first prerequisite for initiating a relationship of love is *trust*. Love entails "placing one's whole self in the hands of the beloved, in whom we fully confide."[2] Love is established upon a foundation of mutual trust and culminates, via reciprocal devotion, with union between the lovers. If one gives, the other receives. Without this *reciprocal gift*, everything will "stall" at a halfway point, and it will be impossible to arrive at that intimate union in which two hearts beat in unison and two souls merge into one.

In the end, trust is itself a form of giving. The word "surrender" has at once an active and a passive sense: It means both giving and yielding. To surrender oneself is to love and to accept love: to give oneself generously and yield oneself trustingly. Trust and giving strengthen each other. To open oneself up confers a certain power upon the other; it entails a risk that only trust in the other's love can persuade one to take. In a good love relationship, there are no secrets. On the other hand, if trust fades, the relationship becomes paralyzed. Faith and fidelity go hand in hand. To have faith in someone means to trust that he or she will be faithful to us. And, as Thibon, observes, "Whoever is incapable of faith is incapable of fidelity."[3]

---

2. Llano, *La Vida Lograda*, p. 112.

3. G. Thibon, *La crisis moderna del amor*, 4th ed. (Barcelona: Fontanella, 1976), p. 70.

Where does mistrust come from? Some are mistrustful simply because of the way they were raised. There are also those who don't trust others because they project their own insecurity onto them. In some individuals, this self-esteem problem stems from past disappointments. Wounded pride can distort reality so much that even an objectively friendly gesture is regarded with suspicion. If such individuals are unable to heal their wounds by cultivating humble self-esteem, they become self-sufficient: it's difficult for them to accept that they need love from others. They may even feel humiliated by the simple fact that someone has offered them help.

In love, we tend to shift between two extremes: surrender and reserve. Pride and fear prevent us from giving or receiving fully. As the protagonist of one of Sándor Márai's novels expresses it:

> It takes a lot of bravery to allow yourself to be loved without reserve. A bravery that is almost heroism. Most people can't either give or receive love because they are cowardly and proud, because they're afraid of failing. They're afraid to offer themselves to another person, and even more afraid to surrender, because they're scared he'll discover their secret . . . the sad secret of every human being: that he needs a lot of tenderness, that he can't live without love.[4]

There are those who hedge their bets and prefer to preserve their immunity to the disturbances of love, but they pay a high price for this. Their lives end in tremendous loneliness.

---

4. S. Márai, *La mujer justa* (Barcelona: Salamandra, 2005), p. 146.

As the French philosopher Gabriel Marcel put it, "Nothing is lost for the man who lives a great love or a true friendship, but all is lost for him who is alone."[5]

To allow oneself to be loved is not a sign of weakness. Acknowledging one's own penury requires a good measure of humility and fortitude. A reluctance to admit our need for love stunts our growth; we remain children at heart. We are weak within, although we conceal it for fear of rejection. Without humble self-esteem, there is no truthfulness—with ourselves or with others. Few dare "to manifest the truth totally, without diminishing or retouching anything, without any measure of more or less fraudulent compromise."[6] Ideally, there should be no difference between the way we really are, the way we think we are, and the way we show ourselves to others. People who hide their weaknesses usually become defensive when their weaknesses come to light. And, as we shall see, it's not easy to remove this iron shell if one has grown accustomed to playing a certain theatrical role, before oneself as much as other audiences. Says the heroine of one of Gaite's novels:

> I sometimes think that people lie out of an inability to cry out, begging people to accept you as you are. When you resist confessing the helplessness of your life, you're already disguising yourself as something else. You start to get the hang of it, and from then on, you're really lost; you're turning somersaults with your mask on, getting further and further away from the road that could lead

---

5. Gabriel Marcel, *Lettre à Roger Troisfontaines* (in reference to his play, *La cœur des autres*, Paris: Grasset, 1921).

6. J. Green, *Libertad querida* (Barcelona: Plaza & Janés, 1990), p. 103.

you to finding out who you are. . . . I notice it more
and more: thirst for appreciation, or however you like to
call it.[7]

Our masks only disappear before someone who truly loves
us. Only then do we act spontaneously. Without a doubt, if
we knew the love of God more deeply from childhood and
lived continually in his presence, we wouldn't spend so much
time performing for others.

IDEAL LOVE AND ITS ATTRIBUTES

Without humble self-esteem, not only is the ability to receive
love compromised, but so is the *purity of intention* and *interior
freedom* in giving love. Because we might be unfamiliar with
these concepts, it is worth examining the elements of an ideal
love. We can look at them first of all in the context of love
between man and woman, though they may also be applied to
other loves: of God, family members, or friends.

The beginnings of love between a man and a woman are
very attractive (some people even become addicted to this),
but they are only preparations for the journey and do not
guarantee the success of the whole voyage. "Falling in love"
is a feeling that doesn't endure. It's a good point of depar-
ture, but it must be transcended in order to grow into a more
mature love. "If love is understood as a mere sentiment,
sooner or later a couple will conclude that they don't love each
other."[8] To the extent that love progresses, its inner elements
become more important than its outer ones. In mockery of
merely sentimental love, Albert Cohen writes:

7. C. Martín Gaite, *Lo raro es vivir* (Barcelona: Anagrama, 1996), p. 149.
8. A. Malo, *Antropologia dell' affettività* (Roma: Armando, 1999), p. 293.

If poor Romeo had suddenly had his nose cut clean off in an accident, when Juliet next saw him she would have run away in horror. Thirty grams less meat and Juliet's soul is no longer nobly stirred. Thirty grams less and that is the end of sublime moonlight babble.[9]

Recent films have accustomed us to conceiving of physical-romantic attraction as the height of love. But they forget (it wouldn't be "dramatically correct") that when this is the case, sadly, love evaporates as easily as it once overpowered used. In the movie *Stepmom*,[10] the protagonist finds himself obliged to explain to his children the reasons for his divorce (his feelings "had changed"). But he didn't expect the reply, voiced with worried curiosity by the littlest one: "You mean you might fall out of love with your children, too?" It was a realistic reflection of the disappointment that frequently ensues when love is confused with passion. "Unfortunately," writes Cronin, "the idea of sexual attraction as the fundamental basis of marriage, drenched in a cloying romanticism and dripping with the false promise of an eternal honeymoon, has become an integral part of the modern dream."[11]

For love to be stable and enduring, one needs to pass from "love as attraction" to "love as donation"—since nothing unites two people so much as the desire of each for the good of the other. In mature love, egocentric motivations disappear, and there is more focus upon opportunities to bring each other happiness. "It is possible for everything to begin with some *reason*," notes Josef Pieper, "but when love has been

---

9. A. Cohen, *Book of My Mother* (New York: Archipelago, 2012), p. 80.

10. Chris Columbus, director; Columbia Pictures, 1998.

11. A. J. Cronin, *Adventures in Two Worlds* (Madrid: Palabra, 1997).

kindled, no reasons are needed."[12] One no longer loves so much for the sake of the beloved's attractions but *for what he or she is*—no longer the "mere physical apparel" so much as the nucleus of the person, "incomparable and irreplaceable."[13] This solid and mature love is imperishable. Whoever experiences it understands Gabriel Marcel's recurrent, celebrated exclamation: "To love a being is to say to him: You will not die."[14] Beyond the boundaries of death, the beloved continues to live within the lover.

While passion is not the most vital element, it shouldn't be excluded, since it nourishes love. Still, as love progresses, the relationship is transformed into "a deep unity, maintained by the will and deliberately strengthened by habit."[15] Passion is accepted and placed at the service of surrender. Love may be compared to an airplane with two engines: a primary one (will) and an auxiliary one (passion). The auxiliary engine may fail regardless of our wishes, due to sickness or fatigue, but the main engine never shuts down without our consent. If the engine of the will is lacking, Thibon observes, "the slightest physical or moral trial suffices to submerge in essential solitude those lovers who are united only by the flesh or by a dream."[16]

We can distinguish three types of human love: enjoyment (which remains at the physical, bodily level), desire

---

12. J. Pieper, *About Love* (Chicago: Franciscan Herald Press, 1974); Spanish edition (Madrid: Rialp, 1972), pp. 102–103.

13. In R. de los Rios, *Cuando el mundo gira enamorado*, 8th edition (Madrid: Rialp, 2009), p. 61.

14. Cf. Ch. Moeller, *Literatura del siglo XX y Cristianismo*, Vol. IV (Madrid: Gredos, 1964), pp. 179–341. See also Jose Luis Cañas, Gabriel Marcel: *Filósofo, Dramaturgo y Compositor* (Madrid: Palabra, 1998).

15. Lewis, *Mere Christianity*, p. 92.

16. Thibon, *La crisis moderna del amor*, p. 123.

(somewhat more emotional, affective, proper to the heart), and love (essentially tied to the spiritual aspect, the soul). Ideally, lovers enjoy each other, love each other, and are good friends as well. Inversely, we can identify three types of egotism: physical (sexual possessiveness), affective (emotional possessiveness), and spiritual (pride). These three spheres also correspond to three types of happiness and unhappiness: good food or a toothache, cheerfulness or emotional clashes, inner peace or a troubled conscience. The more profound the happiness or sadness, the less visible it is from the outside. A toothache is hard to hide, but the loneliness that threatens the soul tends to pass unobserved. Whoever seeks a merely sensory happiness, if he or she succeeds, is not sad but misses out on the greatest joy—the joy of love. In French, the word for "unhappy" is "*malheureux*": literally, "badly happy."

The ideal lover puts all three spheres at the service of the beloved's happiness. Physical attraction and falling in love is, indeed, a fine anteroom to the surrender of all that is most intimate, which will come with time. For this reason it requires a purification that situates it properly. Depending on the soul's dispositions, sexual and affective egotism will be battled, or else will gain ground. A good relationship with oneself, along with the always-gratifying complement of a humble self-esteem, helps to purify one's sexual and affective intentions, whereas the opposite, marred by pride, corrupts passion. Throughout this chapter, the link between pride and affective egotism will grow gradually clearer.

Let us now explore the four properties that determine the quality of love. Ideal love is *sacrificial, disinterested, respectful,* and *free.* Most people aren't accustomed to evaluating their love relationships. These four parameters—which can also be called operative surrender, rectitude of intention, detachment, and interior freedom—so difficult to unite—rise above the usual approach ("How is this courtship, or this marriage, going?") and the usual, simple response ("We get along well; we love each other a lot.")

The first two qualities are linked to the truth, or genuineness, of the love; the last two, to its freedom. Indeed, genuine love is ruled equally by truth and freedom. Love's truth has to do with deeds and intentions: We truly love if we are moved by upright intentions and if our deeds confirm our love. And we love in freedom if we avoid an inner rigidity—if we don't pressure the beloved. One's answers to the following four questions will help determine the quality of a couple's relationship:

1. How much are you willing to sacrifice yourself for the other's happiness?
2. Do you respect the other's freedom, or do you manage things by imposing your own will?
3. What is your real motivation in surrendering yourself?
4. Do you surrender freely, or do you sense an internal pressure?

The perfection of love, then, consists of two visible qualities—capacity for sacrifice and respect for freedom—and two invisible ones—rectitude of intention and interior freedom. We could call this the "body and soul" of love.

Capacity for Sacrifice

The capacity for sacrifice—concrete deeds that contribute to the beloved's good—reveals the authenticity of our love. "Deeds are love, not good intentions," as the saying goes.

When determining if someone genuinely loves us, we should focus on deeds, not intentions. What does the person do to show his love? Does he sacrifice himself for us without regard to his mood, or the effort demanded? Someone who genuinely loves us will be ready for any sacrifice if it adds to our happiness. In principle, we ought to trust in someone's love for us, but we will only be secure to the degree that it is demonstrated with deeds, since "the real proof of affection is given by sacrifice."[17] This is why it's often only in times of adversity that we discover who our real friends are.

Sacrifice, then, reveals the *truth* and also the *intensity* of love. The kind of sacrifice someone makes for us provides information about *how much* he or she loves us. "How much do you love me?" lovers are prone to ask. It's not an easy question to answer. Instead, one would do well to ask, "In times of hardship, what would you be willing to do for me?" Only thus can we tangibly quantify someone's love. We love as much as we're willing to sacrifice. We all have our price.

Respect for Freedom

The second visible feature of ideal love, *respect for the beloved's freedom*, implies first of all not imposing oneself on the beloved. Lack of respect covers a broad spectrum. It ranges from spiritual pressure, like that of an authoritarian mind (regarding style, tastes, and opinions) to sexual pressure—someone who treats the beloved as a mere object of pleasure—and includes affective pressure, like that of someone with a pathological need for endless proofs of affection.

17. J. Escrivá, *The Way of the Cross* (London: Scepter, 2004), 5th station, no. 1.

Affective pressure, or "possessiveness," is characteristic of demanding, jealous people. "He loves me a lot, so much that at times it's oppressive," says one of Gaite's characters.[18] In such cases, everything is possible: imposition, belief in one's exclusive rights to someone, coercion, emotional blackmail, reproaches that are only apparently well-intentioned— anything to impose one's own will. At the other end of the spectrum is "detachment." Later, as we study affectivity, we'll investigate the relation between pride and the possessive urge, between humble self-esteem and affective detachment.

Far from this landscape of shadows, the ideal couple neither gives orders; each obeys. This is the point and counterpoint that respect for freedom offers, a goal as difficult as it is essential for every relationship of love. This is the scenario sketched by Delibes in one of his novels, inspired by his relationship with his late wife.

> Ours was an enterprise of two. One produced and the other distributed. Ordinary, no? She never felt neglected. On the contrary, she had more than enough skill to erect herself as head without overthrowing anybody. She declined the appearance of authority, but she knew how to wield it. I would raise my voice once in a while, but in reality she was the one to resolve, in every case, what to do, or what to stop doing. In every couple, there's an active and a passive element: one who carries things out, and one who paves the way. Although it may not have looked that way, I yielded to her good judgment and accepted her authority.[19]

18. Gaite, *Lo raro es vivir* (Barcelona: Editorial Anagrama, 1999) p. 89.
19. M. Delibes, *Señora de rojo sobre fondo gris* (Barcelona: Destino, 1991), pp. 41–42.

Purity of Intention

Let's take a look now at the first invisible quality of ideal love: *purity of intention*. The same act may be motivated by different intentions. One's motives are pure when they don't place one's own advantage ahead of the good of the beloved. "To love" is the opposite of "to use."[20] The utilitarian individual takes advantage of the beloved to the extent that he or she gives with the sole aim of receiving. It's worth making some distinctions here, though, to avoid all possible ambiguity. "It's not a question of going on a fanatical and scrupulous hunt for the absence of all *interest*," explains Carlos Cardona, "but of preserving a duly ordered hierarchy."[21] Human beings are not capable of an absolutely disinterested love: for one thing, because we need to receive love in order to be perfected. Only God, who lacks nothing, is capable of entirely gratuitous love. What can rightly be required of us, though, are *sincere intentions*: that we don't consciously swindle anyone by concealing egotistical motives.

Purity of intention doesn't merely indicate a momentary desire to avoid seeking our own advantage; it is a capacity we acquire little by little as we progress in virtue. Apart from those clearly egotistical motives that lead us to use others, there are other, deeper (and therefore less conscious) ones that also cloud the uprightness of our actions. For instance, it isn't easy to control "background defects" such as vanity or self-love. To ensure a right intention at this level, a thorough inner purification is needed, so that the degree of disinterest in our actions gradually increases as we grow in perfection.

---

20. See Karol Wojtyła, *Love and Responsibility* (San Francisco: Ignatius, 1993).
21. C. Cardona, *Metafísica del bien y del mal* (Pamplona: EUNSA, 1987), p. 129.

Interior Freedom

The second invisible quality of love is *interior freedom*. Freedom, more than action, is a *capacity for self-determination*. I am not free simply because no one is forcing me to do something; freedom means that I am capable of *doing things because I choose to*. In other words, freedom has as much to do with the absence of a certain inner coercion as the absence of external force. Some, for want of generosity, don't know how to say yes; others, for want of firm character, don't know how to say no. Sometimes they complain that others don't respect their freedom, when in reality the trouble is that they themselves don't know how to be free.

The mature person doesn't allow himself to be pushed around, but he is capable of surrendering his own liberty out of love, since he is master of it. He always knows how *to be himself*: he feels interiorly free of other people and circumstances. He is beyond the reach of external pressures. *It's not that he does whatever he feels like doing, but rather that he feels like choosing to do good.* Freedom is the capacity for self-determination: preferably towards goodness, and better still when motivated by love, not duty. This is why the truly free person is the one who *internalizes* the good rather than being motivated by an obsession with duty. Out of love, he identifies his own will with that of the beloved.

Indeed, love best illustrates interior freedom. We're able to give ourselves freely to others to the degree that we're masters of ourselves. To love is to freely belong to another. The egotistical lover seeks to *possess* the beloved; by contrast, the ideal lover desires above all to *belong to him*. Love is "not to belong to oneself, but to be happily and freely, with heart and soul, subject to another's will . . . and at the same time to one's

own."[22] But in order for the will of the other to coincide with
one's own, one needs to possess oneself before belonging to
the other. If, for want of inner freedom, one isn't master of
oneself, one ends up yielding in a servile manner. This, in the
long run, will satisfy neither oneself nor the beloved. Only
truly mature persons are capable of binding themselves in love
with complete inner freedom.

Inner freedom is rooted in maturity, but the chief source
by which it is nourished is love, because love implies a harmony with the desires of the beloved. People who love each
other identify with each other's wills; they "share a horizon."
This "freedom of love"[23] helps to clarify St. Augustine's phrase,
"Love and do as you will." Whoever ardently desires the good
of the beloved acts freely and gladly, not sparing any effort to
make the beloved happy.

In sum, love is a mutual, free, and disinterested yielding
of the most intimate depth of the self, between an "I" and a
"thou." One of the best definitions of love is this: "To love
means to give and receive something which can be neither
bought nor sold, but only given freely and mutually."[24]

PRIDE AND THE QUALITY OF LOVE

The invisible qualities of ideal love, inner freedom, and
purity of intention are harder to achieve than the visible ones,
capacity for sacrifice and respect for the beloved. It's easier to
improve the "body" (the visible element) than the "soul" (the

---

22. J. Escrivá, *Furrow* (New York: Scepter, 1992), no. 797.
23. Cf. J. Escrivá, *Way of the Cross*, 10th station.
24. John Paul II, *Letter to Families*, February 2, 1994, no. 11.

invisible element). Uprightness of intention and interior free-dom are the fruits of an arduous spiritual conquest.[25] Will-power is insufficient to attain them; much humble self-esteem is needed as well. Those who have a poor relationship with themselves, if they are very strong-willed, can, perhaps, sacri-fice themselves and respect others' freedom, but they will run into great difficulty when it comes to resisting self-seeking or giving themselves "just because they feel like it." Superficially, all seems well, but eventually difficulties rooted in pride are bound to arise.

Humble self-esteem is indispensable for progress in love. Without it, all the qualities of ideal love remain in doubt or are weakened. When we analyze the phenomenon of vol-untarism, we'll see how pride can pervert generosity in sac-rifice. Respect for others' freedom also diminishes if humble self-esteem is lacking. The origin of possessiveness often lies in a certain fear of not measuring up, a doubt of one's own worth. If this thirst for appreciation is not kept under con-trol, affection degenerates into oversensitivity and abuse, since those dissatisfied with themselves tend to feel a great need to monopolize others.

Pride also compromises the invisible qualities of love. We've already seen how freedom is nourished not only by love but also by the maturity typical of people "comfortable in their own skin." Finally, pride tarnishes purity of intention. People

---

25. Experience shows that genuine love is not merely the result of a vigorous spir-itual battle. As I have already indicated, and as we'll see in more depth in the second part of this book, true maturity is also a gift (a grace) to be received. In reality, only the saints are capable of surrendering themselves entirely freely and disinterestedly. To achieve an optimal relationship with ourselves, we need to expe-rience an unconditional love. Supernatural maturity is thus the best complement of human maturity.

plagued by self-doubt have such a need for appreciation that they tend to behave well with the sole aim of securing it. But overly confident people can also be driven by intentions that are less than pure. This happens when we allow ourselves to be led by that "somewhat questionable zeal to help others in order to convince ourselves of our superiority."[26]

Self-sufficient persons know how to give but not how to receive—their generosity has an element of vanity to it. Though they may seem obliging, they gaze at themselves through a flattering lens. They serve their neighbor in order to feel comfortable with themselves; they do favors for others to prove their own goodness. This way of giving recalls what Chateaubriand said of his friend Joubert: "He's a perfect egotist: he thinks only of others . . . "[27] In reality, this is pure self-complacency. It is therefore inaccurate to assert without qualification that the generous person is the one who gives, while the egotist is the one who receives. The art of loving requires *generosity in giving* and also *humility in receiving.* It's hard to say which of these virtues is the more accessible. What's clear is that a relationship of love only works if reciprocity is present. If one doesn't know how to receive, the other can't give.

Additionally, the self-sufficient person may know how to *give*, but not how to *give of self.* Love is the art of giving oneself as one gives something, and of giving something as one gives oneself. The gift of something invisible (myself, my person) needs a visible vehicle to express it. To manifest our love, we can buy a material gift for the beloved, for example. But at the same time, this gift itself may be corrupt. Any "donation"

---

26. J. Escrivá, *Friends of God*, no. 230.
27. In C. Pujol, *Siete escritores conversos* (Madrid: Palabra, 1994), p. 31.

implies the surrender of something intimate. Self-sufficiency *gives* but does not *give of itself*; it does favors, but with a certain coldness; it does not commit its own inner self.

This unwholesome independence clouds a relationship of love; to enjoy a higher level of love, one must, without exception, cultivate both an *excellent personality* and a *great affective capacity*. The greatest loves are the ones between mature persons who love each other deeply. They are wholesomely *independent*, having definitively conquered any problems of self-esteem, and lovingly *dependent*, each wishing only to make the other happy. Thus, in an ideal marriage, both spouses manage to reconcile human maturity and affective generosity, and each can say to each other: "In a certain sense, I don't care what you think of me; in another, I'm consumed by the desire to make you happy."

Dependence and Independence

Experience teaches us that we can't depend exclusively on others to gauge our personal worth. The importance of others' opinions becomes more and more diluted as self-knowledge increases. We grow familiar with our abilities and limitations and learn to accept them. There is, however, a hidden danger inherent in this process that can throw off the equilibrium we've reached with others. This occurs when one equates maturity with a lack of interest in others. It is a mistake to think that dependence on others is an obstacle to self-realization. This approach leads, in practice, not to the achievement of legitimate personal independence but to a sterile victory, through cold unconcern, over one's dependencies. It doesn't lead to independence—only indifference. True independence isn't born of coldness or distance but of inner freedom and the ability to love with detachment. It's one thing not to depend on the opinion of others; it's quite another to disregard them. As we grow in perfection, we acquire the freedom that allows us to combine a healthy independence *and* a healthy dependence. They don't preclude each other, though at first glance they may seem to. The balanced person is at once sensitive and strong. He or she has the kindness to say yes but doesn't lack the personality to calmly say no. Maturity harmonizes these two aspects; this is why we admire those whose affection makes them vulnerable but whose sense of dignity makes them strong. They're capable of gladly accepting the bonds love creates; at the same time, their humble self-esteem allows them to preserve a wholesome independence. The opposite provokes rejection—those fragile people who require constant attentions (infantilism) as well as the arrogant ones who won't accept help or love from anyone (individualism).

We could call the synthesis of independence and dependence *"auto-dependence."*[28] It involves the avoidance of both false dependencies and false independence. False *dependence* leads to a servile frame of mind. We witness this in insecure people who, for fear of being disliked, are afraid to say no. False *independence*, on the other hand, denotes self-sufficiency and egotism. We observe this in those somewhat arrogant people who wash their hands of others. Whereas a servile attitude stems from a lack of interior freedom, the desire to preserve one's autonomy at all costs comes of an erroneous conception of freedom. Freedom is not worth much unless it can be surrendered for the sake of love.

False independence is far more harmful than false dependence. Calling attention to oneself is preferable to pretending

---

28. J. Bucay, *El camino a la autodependencia* (Barcelona: Grijalbo, 2002).

to need no one. Self-sufficiency isolates us from others; vanity at least leads us to take them into account. Loving badly is preferable to not loving at all. "Vanity," Lewis argues,

> though it is the sort of Pride which shows most on the surface, is really the least bad and most pardonable sort. The vain person wants praise, applause, admiration, too much and is always angling for it. It is a fault, but a childlike and even (in an odd way) a humble fault. It shows that you are not yet completely contented with your own admiration. You value other people enough to want them to look at you. You are, in fact, still human. The real black, diabolical Pride comes when you look down on others so much that you do not care what they think of you. Of course, it is very right, and often our duty, not to care what people think of us, if we do so for the right reason; namely, because we care so incomparably more what God thinks. But the Proud man has a different reason for not caring. He says, "Why should I care for the applause of that rabble? . . . [A]m I the sort of man to blush with pleasure at a compliment like some chit of a girl at her first dance? No, I am an integrated, adult personality."[29]

In practice, both self-sufficiency and vanity are hard to avoid. Only the saints manage to attain it fully. They experience what St. Paul affirms: "For though I am free from all men, I have made myself a slave to all . . ." (1 Cor 9:19). The rest of us, given our limitations, strive for balance and manage as best we can. Some, for fear of losing their autonomy, won't surrender to anybody and end up living in solitude; others,

---

29. Lewis, *Mere Christianity*, p. 72.

beset by an insatiable hunger for affirmation, go about with heart in hand and bind themselves in a servile manner to the first bidder. Based on these reflections, we will now delve into the complex world of affectivity and explore its relation to the quality of love, self-esteem, and the spiritual faculties of intellect and will.

THE HEART'S ENERGIES

Nothing makes us more dependent, in the best and the worst sense, than affection. The heart is a double-edged sword. Its good side is its *discernment* and *capacity for sacrifice*; its bitter side, its *injustice* and *possessiveness*. At its best, affection sharpens ingenuity[30] and lends wings to the will. At its worst, it thwarts common sense and detachment. Emotional maturity requires continual adjustments and rebalancing. At the level of intelligence, affective passion facilitates empathy, but it can also blind the reason. Affectivity fosters two hearts beating in sync, but vehement passion impedes that "natural sense of reserve which everyone finds attractive because it denotes intelligent self-control."[31] Thanks to affection, a mother grasps immediately how her child is feeling, but that fondness can also cloud her judgment and lead to all sorts of irrational behavior. The will is like a two-sided coin: affection facilitates generosity, especially when sacrifice is called for, but it also fuels possessive tendencies.

---

30. According to Thomas Aquinas, perfect knowledge is "affective knowledge of the truth" (*Summa Theologiae*, II-II, q. 162, a. 3 ad 1). The classical thinkers distinguished between *intellect* and *reason*: to be *intelligent* is broader than to be *reasonable*.

31. J. Escrivá, *Friends of God*, no. 84.

The heart is at once powerful and fragile. It is able to persevere in adversity, but it becomes vulnerable in the face of indifference. The sensitive person, unless he purifies his affections, suffers from an excessive need to feel loved. If he lacks other resources, he is exposed to painful disappointments. His fortitude breaks down easily. The more his self-esteem deteriorates and the more his sadness grows, the greater his tendency to demand affirmation and encourage his own fantasies. His blind desire to see his value affirmed bodes ill for the future. He appears headed for a dead end, caught between the affective expectations he's nourished with his imagination and the real impossibility of satisfying such an excessive thirst for attention.

But we will leave the negative aspects of affectivity for the next section and focus first on the profound benefits it offers. The heart is the motor that moves one to love, to give oneself. "Take note," observes Antonio Machado. "A heart alone is no heart at all."[32] If the heart is brimming with affection, all its strength will be poured into the desire to procure happiness for the beloved, never counting the cost. And if happiness is attained, it amply compensates for any suffering or effort. The *bliss of making someone happy* is proportionate to the affection involved.

In a mature person, heart and will buttress each other. Above all, "to love is to will the good of another."[33] Love resides in the will, but when the heart helps, the surrender "runs smoothly." Otherwise, if affection is reticent and self-donation becomes arduous, the "motor" of the will supplies what is lacking to make a *glad* sacrifice, even if *without inclination*. Even if the heart is *cold*, the will inflames it.

---

32. A. Machado, *Canciones*, no. LXVI.
33. Thomas Aquinas, *On Charity*, art. 7.b.

"The perfection of the moral good consists in man's being moved to the good not only by his will but also by his 'heart.'"[34] Goodness ought to impregnate the intellect, the will, and the heart. As Alejandro Llano states:

> A good character formation is one that leads me to a liking for good and a dislike for evil. For this would be a sign that my freedom is leaving its mark on my very body, that a sense for what is right is being infused into the substance of my blood. Thus I can succeed in overcoming the schizophrenia, so common today, between the cold rationalism that dominates Monday through Friday and the fever of dispersion that takes over on the weekend. I begin to attain a single life, though not a univocal or monotonous one. I gradually integrate into my life those goods that are found at the roots of my own personality. The poetry of the heart begins to penetrate the prose of the intellect.[35]

It's a question of pooling our resources—intellect, will, and affectivity—and placing them at the service of love. The intellect inspires good intentions, and the will, sustained by the heart, puts them into practice.

The goodness that can radiate from the heart is astonishing. "Everything I've ever done in my life, in all different fields, I've done out of affection," said Eduardo Ortiz de Landázuri.[36] Many parents, especially mothers, could say the

---

34. *Catechism of the Catholic Church*, 1775.

35. Llano, *La Vida Lograda*, p. 79.

36. In E. López-Escobar and P. Lozano, *Eduardo Ortiz de Landázuri* (Madrid: Palabra, 1994), p. 279. This university professor, admired for his medical knowledge and his sanctity, died in 1985. In 1998, his process of beatification was initiated.

same. "Admirable strength of maternal love, holy glimmer of divine love that finds strength for all things and never tires of the most unbearable sacrifice and weariness!"[37] At first glance, the insensitive person appears stronger, but in the long run he or she is less persevering in adversity. The capacity for self-denial in magnanimous people, by contrast, is striking. Perhaps, superficially, they succumb when faced with minor contradictions, but when confronted with great sorrow they show greater strength of character. We see this most of all in women. They are capable of the greatest sacrifice—as long as they feel cherished. "Give a woman love, and there is nothing she won't do, suffer, or risk," proclaims Wilkie Collins.[38]

The heart also adds a human touch to our surroundings. We notice it when it's absent, for example in the workplace and the arena of economics, where calculations, facts, and figures are more highly valued than respect for personal dignity. An absence of the "human factor" leads people to focus on things, not persons, and to sacrifice the *important* for the *urgent*. This framework helps us to understand Gabriel Marcel's celebrated distinction between *being* and *having*.[39] The world of *having* corresponds to objective realities like technology, where no communication is possible, only solitude and emptiness, with the human being reduced to a mere function. By contrast, the world of *being* is the world of being available to one another, of authentic communication and transcendence.

Apart from the world of work, family life and social relations are often contaminated by the lack of a human touch.

37. E. Gil y Carrasco, *El Señor de Bembibre* (Madrid: Rialp, 1999), p. 103.
38. Wilkie Collins, *La ley y la dama*, 6th edition (Madrid: Rialp, 2007), p. 20.
39. Cf. Marcel, *Ser y Tener* (Madrid: Guadarrama, 1971).

One sees this, for example, in distinguished families in which courtesy has degenerated into empty formality, for want of warmth. "This soul-chilling coldness often pervades especially refined environments, turning fellowship itself into something artificial."[40] Even a misguided conception of Christianity can lead to an "official charity, something dry and soulless."[41] In either case, as Marcel puts it, a world in which interpersonal relationships have disappeared leads to a "suffocating sorrow."[42]

DETACHED AFFECTION AMONG FRIENDS

Ideal affection is *detached*. It leads to the realization that loving someone does not oblige him or her to love us in return—and that therefore any attempt at forcing a response is senseless. Real affection is therefore subtle in its suggestions and kind in its "signals." An anecdote can illustrate this "art of not imposing oneself." There was a young man who was deeply in love with a girl who, because of her own insecurity, and despite a lengthy courtship, had not reached the point of commitment. The young man asked a mutual friend of theirs for a favor:

> If you happen to hear her say she's planning to leave me, please let me know: that way I'll be able to spare her a bad time. I'll send her a card to say thank you for everything, and I'll tell her good-bye forever . . . My main objective is to make her happy, but if she doesn't love me, I'll never be able to do it . . .

40. M. A. Martí García, *La afectividad* (Madrid: Ediciones Internacionales Universitarias, 2000), p. 43.
41. J. Escrivá, *Christ Is Passing By*, no. 167.
42. See G. Marcel, *Le monde cassé* (Paris: Desclée de Brouwer, 1933).

This is a true example of respect and rectitude of intention.

At the other end of the spectrum is possessiveness, which masks a thousand forms of egotism. This imperfect love is "a sort of egocentric self-affirmation."[43] It can be explained (though not justified). Lewis relates it to "affection's need to be needed."[44] Hidden beneath this possessiveness is often a clamor to feel useful, a blind desire to affirm one's own value, the subject of a morbid uncertainty, or a thousand manifestations of the fear of rejection. It's a puzzle, interwoven with both legitimate wounds of the heart and the effects of pride. "What deep suffering we can inflict on those who love us, and how awful is our power to hurt them," says Albert Cohen, recalling his late mother.[45] When reflecting on our sorrows, in order to distinguish the good from evil that the heart brings upon us, we must learn to distinguish between a *wounded heart* and *wounded pride*. If someone we love despises us, it may pain us—not only in our heart but also in our pride. If it were only a matter of the heart, the pain would be legitimate. We wouldn't get angry; at most we would suffer in silence. Self-love, by contrast, engenders oversensitivity.

The danger of growing possessive is present in all forms of love—between friends, lovers, parents, and children—but it increases in tandem with the intensity of affection. For this reason, detachment is more frequent between friends than between lovers, although it's more meritorious between people united by powerful bonds of affection. We will spend some time on this *love of friendship* because of a certain quality that

43. D. von Hildebrand, *The Heart* (South Bend, Ind.: St. Augustine Press, 2012); Spanish edition: (Madrid: Palabra, 1997), p. 129.

44. C.S. Lewis, *The Four Loves* (New York: Houghton Mifflin Harcourt, 1941), p. 51.

45. A. Cohen, *Book of My Mother* (Brooklyn, NY: Archipelago Books, 2012), p. 66.

serves as a model for other types of human love. The ideal is that couples who are madly in love avoid possessiveness, taking inspiration from the behavior of good friends.

The Greeks long ago distinguished between friendship (*philia*) and falling in love (*eros*). *Eros* can arise unexpectedly and create great dependency. Friendship, on the other hand, is the product of a free decision (hence the Latin term *dilectio*, which comes from *electio*). According to Cicero, friendship stems more from "nature herself" than from a feeling of need.[46] True friendship, affirms C.S. Lewis, is ruled by freedom: it is a "luminous, tranquil, rational world of relationships freely chosen."[47] For this reason, it is "the least jealous of loves . . . the least biological."[48] Common affinities facilitate mutual understanding, but true friendship doesn't arise as a product of particular interests, nor is it preserved because of interests created. If the friends have reached the level of this type of love, they meet at a point of indifference about the details, the affections, and the frankly expressed truths, and any enormous differences are as respected as they are unbridgeable. Indeed, there's an opportunity for continual progress and mutual enrichment. Given the depth of this type of love, the famous words that American Mary Haskell wrote to her great friend, the Lebanese poet Kahlil Gibran, ten years her junior, when, from the tone of a recent letter, she found that he had fallen in love with her: "Let us not allow this beautiful friendship to be degraded by turning it into a vulgar love affair."[49]

46. M. T. Cicero, *On Friendship* (New York, The Century Company, 1901), p. 46.

47. Lewis, *The Four Loves*, p. 59.

48. Lewis, *The Four Loves*, pp. 57–58

49. In H. Arts, *De wegen van het hart: Over vriendschap* (Louvain: Davidsfonds, 1991), p. 12.

Cicero defined friendship as "harmony of opinion and sentiment about all things human and divine, with mutual good-will and affection."[50] Good friends, then, are those who understand, love, and respect each other. Mutual understanding is a distinctive trait of friendship, whereas affection and benevolence are essential elements of all forms of love. The classic term "benevolence," which has fallen out of general use, is especially interesting with regard to our reflections on the quality of love, since it implies three of the qualities of ideal love: respect, purity of intention, and interior freedom. Applied to the subject at hand, benevolence is the corrective of which affection stands in need. Thanks to the virtue of benevolence, affection grows respectful, detached, and disinterested.

Regarding mature love, I've distinguished between *love as attraction* and *love as giving*. Analogously, the classical thinkers set *concupiscence* against *benevolence*, indicating that someone driven by imperious necessity will not be able to conduct himself or herself with benevolence. They recall that only God, who lacks nothing, is perfectly benevolent. In other words, in order to be able to give, one must have. A rich person is more able than a needy one to give alms freely and disinterestedly. Applying this to love, we can understand why detachment is so characteristic of people who, thanks to humble self-esteem, have attained a high moral perfection. "Virtue," contends Cicero, "both begets and preserves friendships."[51] Virtue consists of mutual agreement, stability, and consistency of conduct and character. Once again, humble self-esteem proves to be the solution. Only with its help can one increase one's own

---

50. Cicero, *On Friendship*, p. 33.
51. Cicero, *On Friendship*, p. 34.

affective capacity and break down the pride that so often poisons the affections. Only then can we say that affection can never be too great.

There are similarities between harmonizing intense affection and detachment on the one hand, and reconciling dependence and independence on the other. Most people are either very affectionate but excessively dependent or independent but cold. Instead of purifying their affections, some are detached but silence their own hearts; others are sensitive but monopolize those they love. The former grow indifferent, the latter oversensitive. Only the saints manage to combine the most intense affection with the most exquisite detachment. "I don't ask you to take away my feelings, Lord," wrote St. Josemaría Escrivá, "because I can use them to serve you with, but I ask you to put them through the crucible."[52] This tried and tested affection, at once powerful and prudent, is so rare that it often gives rise to misunderstandings. Some mistake delicacy for coldness. Edith Stein, for example, who cultivated so many friendships, recounts in a letter that she experienced a love "so pure it was almost not of this world. . . . In my dealings with friends and even with my very family, I have always wanted to do everything out of love, and I believe they understand it that way, although there are perhaps moments when they suspect something else, a certain indifference that in fact is not present."[53]

In short, in order for those united by powerful bonds of affection to love with the same detachment as good friends, they must purify their hearts. Passion is not, in itself, either

---

52. Escrivá, *The Forge* (New York: Scepter, 2002), no. 750.
53. In E. T. Gil de Moro, *Conversaciones con Edith Stein* (Burgos: Monte Carmelo, 2007), p. 155.

good or bad. The heart always has a card to play, but if it is not to betray us it needs a spiritual corrective. The struggle is finding the balance between affection and an inordinate dependence upon it. Instead of "shrinking" the heart to avoid possible trouble, one ought to purify it, restraining its possessive tendencies. Pride is like a hidden virus that contaminates the affections from within. Humble self-esteem is the best treatment—the healthiest path to detached affection. The dreaded fear of rejection, which so wounds our pride, will then disappear. It's not wise to be led by the heart alone, but we should make the most of its riches. Our motto could be "Always with the heart, but never *only* with the heart!"

Let's look at one final question: if we haven't purified our intentions, which is preferable: to love much but badly, or little but well? Faced with this dilemma, some respond like the last princess of the Ottoman court who, as an adolescent, wrote in her diary, "Ah! We're always guilty, either for not loving enough, or for loving too much!" Her mother had tried to educate her affections by harsh treatment, but she didn't understand. She didn't realize that her possessiveness was related precisely to the great affection she felt for her mother. "If I could love her less," wrote the daughter, "and not be so awkward, so anxious to please her, if I could act indifferent. . . . Then she would love me, I'm sure."[54]

Faced with the danger of possessiveness arising from affection, especially passionate affection, it's no wonder that some develop a systematic distrust of the heart. They are overwhelmed by unsatisfied emotional needs and prefer a "preemptive cure." Finding no solution to the problem, they decide to

---

54. K. Mourad, *De parte de la princesa muerta* (Barcelona: Muchnik, 1988), p. 175.

avoid it altogether by "shrinking" their heart. Regarding this aversion to emotion, Miguel Angel Martí writes:

> I've always distrusted those who, moved by who knows what hidden reasons, argue against "sentimentalism," without noticing that their own coldness condemns them. These are people who listen only to the call of duty and whose only norm of conduct is discipline, ignoring their own affective dimension and, naturally, everybody else's, too.[55]

VOLUNTARISM

If the heart atrophies, a crucial source of energy for self-surrender is gone, and the will, stripped of affection, is destined for *voluntarism*—an overemphasis on will to the exclusion of the intellect and heart. Those who aspire to a high degree of moral and Christian perfection are especially susceptible to this.

The will is not the problem; an overemphasis on it is. To understand this, we need to analyze the human being as a whole. We have three equally significant elements at our disposal to measure the quality of a person's love: the heart, the intellect, and the will. The ideal is the ability to possess all three at once: the sensitivity of a poet, the reasoning abilities of a philosopher, and the willpower of an athletic champion. These three elements contribute equally to a harmonious whole. However, any of the three can become inflated, to the detriment of the other two. The three possible deviations are *sentimentalism, intellectualism,* and *voluntarism.* If, however,

---

55. M. A. Martí García, *La afectividad*, p. 29.

the three elements are in harmony, all is well. Love is able to unite all our affective, intellectual, and volitional resources. But we've already seen how the heart, for instance, can disrupt the activities of intellect and will when it leaves its subsidiary role and absorbs or takes over the other spheres.

> The intellect, the will, and the heart ought to cooperate among themselves, each respecting the role and the specific scope of the others. Neither the intellect nor the will should attempt to offer what only the heart can give. And the heart should not arrogate to itself the role of the intellect or the will.[56]

Voluntarism consists of the belief that everything can be gained by sheer effort, despising both the affections' resources and the reasons the intellect can contribute. In the Christian life an overemphasis on the will leads to thrusting supernatural resources to the background, including the inestimable aid of grace. However, the undervaluing of other resources is not something that happens suddenly, nor is it the consequence of a conscious and deliberate process. It happens, little by little, even in those people of impeccable conduct, admirable for their vigor and sense of responsibility. These individuals must learn that, in the game of life, the intellect and the heart play on the same team as the will, regardless of the genetic stamp one is born with. Valuing the heart's strength is important for everyone, but especially for those who by temperament are short on emotional capacity. In this connection, we might recall married couples where fidelity is maintained without love, or people who have surrendered their lives to God but have not yet fallen in love with him.

---

56. D. von Hildebrand, *The Heart*, p. 106.

In both cases the cause may be simply ignorance of the fact that the heart and intellect have as central a role as the will in the growth of love. In both cases, it is important to emphasize this positively, with the utmost delicacy. When helping someone afflicted with voluntarism, it's more important to offer a solution than to focus on the defect. Otherwise, the damage inflicted can be enormous.

A dependence upon one's own efforts is not merely a problem of resources. It's also a question of pride, which affects the quality of one's ability to love, since it doesn't fit in well with inner freedom or rectitude of intention. Deprived of the inspiration and source of strength that these two invisible qualities of love could offer, the victim of voluntarism is destined to turn something as positive as *the desire for perfection* into something as negative as *perfectionism*. The same thing happens with the sense of duty when it is blinded by rigorous self-denial. Indeed, voluntarism is "cured" by employing all the available resources and cultivating humble self-esteem.

Voluntarism can seem to "work" for a while, but it generally ends badly, like a tree with infected roots. It must be gradually corrected or it will degenerate more and more. To love by dint of the will is possible, but it's wearying and demotivating, draining love itself of its meaning. Nature has its unavoidable imperatives: We are made for the happiness of loving, much and well. The voluntarist, by contrast, makes a great effort, but doesn't love well. It's been said that God forgives always, human beings sometimes, and nature never. For this reason, people subjected to great inner tension tend to end up suffering from nervous pathology or psychosomatic illness. If the soul sickens, the body expresses it. Fortunately, these times of crisis can be the catalyst for profound change. The imperatives of the will can find a more pleasant channel when there is room for them to be guided by the heart and the intellect as well. When a house collapses, that's the time to rebuild it upon a stronger foundation.

In any case, the danger of voluntarism is no excuse to stop aspiring to a desire for perfection. It's better to aspire to perfection "incorrectly" than to be idly indifferent. Such aspirations need to be purified so that this imperfect stage of love can be transcended. Certainly, it's preferable to do the good out of a mere sense of duty than not to do it at all, but it's more conducive to perfection—and easier—to sacrifice oneself for the happiness of those we love.

Every great ideal requires effort—sometimes heroic effort. This is true of love, and it is true of the Christian struggle for holiness. All the saints have lived the virtues to a heroic degree, but they know that *holiness*, the perfection of love, is not the same thing as *heroism*. Every saint is heroic, but not every hero is a saint. Both sacrifice themselves for an ideal, but the saint's ideal is love. The hero surrenders himself for something, the saint for Someone. Both perform deeds of valor, but the hero's motivation is not necessarily free of self-love. The saint, on the other hand, aware of his dignity as a child of God, purifies that love, thus growing capable of self-sacrifice—for the Lord or for others—in a more disinterested way. He recalls that "God looks not so much at the greatness of the deeds, nor even at the degree of difficulty, so much as the love with which they are done. . . ."[57] The saint doesn't need to do good deeds out of self-complacency, since the love he receives from God reconciles him with himself. He is in love with the Lord and he intuits that Jesus needs more

---

57. Thérèse of Lisieux, *The Story of the Soul*, 3rd ed. (Washington, DC: ICS Publications, 1996)

"Simons of Cyrene"—co-redeemers to alleviate his redemptive sufferings. This is why every sacrifice, even the most heroic, seems to him small to give joy to his Lord.

LEARNING TO COMMUNICATE

This sketch of ideal love would be incomplete if we failed to touch on problems of communication, if only briefly. The success of a marriage doesn't depend solely on the quality of spousal love. Experience shows that to crown marital life with success, it's not enough to work to increase the depth of that love; the couple must also learn to communicate. In fact, I've known couples that couldn't get along, despite being— individually—truly admirable in their capacity for love. The conclusion is clear: Loving each other isn't sufficient; spouses must also *understand* each other. It's painful to see how poor communication so often contributes to the progressive deterioration of a marriage, with a never-ending series of misunderstandings that could have been avoided by simply being better prepared.

Men and women have equal dignity but different outlooks on life. According to some studies, 80 percent of women consider the level of communication achieved in their marriages to be deficient, compared to just 20 percent of men. Similarly, disappointment in love seems to be more acute among women, whether due to idealism or greater constancy of affection. We could say that women are naturally inclined to focus on what is truly important: giving and receiving love. This is their most decisive source of self-esteem, which is not to say they lack a suitable (though secondary) appreciation for professional success. In one of Wilkie Collins' novels, a discontented wife echoes this reality when she writes to a friend:

I'll tell you what I've observed from experience. Newly married girls who love their husbands deeply—as you do—tend to make a very serious mistake: as a rule, they expect too much of their husbands. Men, my poor Sara, are not like us. Their love, even when it's sincere, isn't like ours; it's not as constant and faithful as what we offer them; it's not their only hope or the reason for their lives, as it is for us.[58]

Generalizations are risky: in every attempt to encompass all of reality, there is room for innumerable distinctions. We're all acquainted, for instance, with men of exquisite sensitivity and women who place their professional work above all else. Nonetheless, it's possible to identify the most common tendencies without refusing to acknowledge the rarer ones. Thus, in general, women, like all sensitive people, understand problems of insecurity better: in Gaite's words, they are "more affected by the absence of love than men, more tormented by the search for an identity that allows them to be valued by others and by themselves."[59] If a woman doesn't feel comfortable in her own skin, she'll be afraid of failing to please others. "To please anyone else, she has to please herself."[60] In his personal diary, Baudouin of Belgium, a king who radiated a certain aura of holiness, prayed regarding his wife as follows: "Teach me to love her tenderly. Give her a more positive vision of herself. May she know that she is loved by You with a love of predilection."[61]

---

58. W. Collins, *La ley y la dama*, p. 153.

59. Gaite, *Cuentos completos*, Prólogo (Madrid: Alianza Editorial, 1981), p. 8.

60. J. M. Contreras, *Pequeños secretos de la vida en común* (Barcelona: Planeta, 1999), p. 86.

61. In Cardinal L. I. Suenens, *Le Roi Baudouin: Une vie que nous parle* (Ertvelde: F.I.A.T., 1995), p. 67.

For both men and women, it's vital to cultivate a good relationship with oneself, which will allow one to develop good relationships with others, too. Men, though different from women in so many respects, also have their way of claiming the appreciation due them, and they, too, need to rightly understand self-love in order to mature in the truth— although they may consider such questions to be secondary. John Gray highlights this point: "A man's deepest fear is that he is not good enough or that he is incompetent. He compensates for this fear by focusing on increasing his power and competence. Success, achievement, and efficiency are foremost in his life."[62] This fear is real, and comes down, in many cases, to insecurity disguised as self-sufficiency—although, as Susana Tamaro puts it in one of her novels, "beneath their apparent arrogance, beneath their apparent security, men are extremely fragile."[63]

It's true that men *seem* more self-confident, but it's equally true that, when threatened by loneliness, they fall into alcoholism or even suicide more frequently than women. If a marriage is going badly, the husband tends to close himself off in his work, whereas the wife—since her self-esteem is more strongly tied to love—is more imaginative in finding ways to continue loving. This explains why, after a disappointment in her marriage, a woman will often throw herself more intensely into her relationship with her children.

However, some disappointments on the part of a wife lack an objective basis: Despite what she thinks, her husband does love her. Sometimes the problem is one of two equally

---

62. John Gray, *Men are from Mars, Women are from Venus* (New York: HarperCollins, 2004), p. 56.
63. S. Tamaro, *Donde el corazón te lleve* (Barcelona: Seix Barral, 1995), p. 108.

negative variables: the lack of self-esteem and the absence of real communication.

Lack of self-esteem develops because a woman "is particularly vulnerable to the negative and incorrect belief that she doesn't deserve to be loved."[64] The more she suffers from self-doubt, the more likely she is to doubt her husband's love. She is unaware that her fear of rejection stems from the same doubts she harbors about her own lovability. The tendency of such women—and of some especially sensitive men—corroborates Cicero's statement about friendship: "There are some who give their friends trouble by imagining that they are held in low esteem, which, however, is not apt to be the case except with those who think meanly of themselves."[65]

Regarding the second cause—flawed communication—a few distinctions are in order. In general, a man is satisfied with *knowing* he is loved, whereas a woman needs to *feel* loved. This is why a woman is more likely to be convinced of her husband's love if she sees him weep for her than if he explains, with cold argumentation, that his love is real. One's approach to housework, such a frequent bone of contention, illustrates this. A man sees his wife singlehandedly doing the chores; this induces him to help out more, not realizing that she would prefer instead a gesture of appreciative companionship. His wife, who has different expectations, doesn't give him credit for his help, which she views as sporadic and unpredictable: she's hoping for other, more convincing proofs of his affection. Common sense invites us to find some way for these two different souls to meet in the middle. Many marital conflicts could be avoided if overly sensitive women learned to place

64. Gray, *Men are from Mars*, p. 53.
65. Cicero, *On Friendship*, p. 72.

more importance on knowing than feeling, and especially virile men made a greater effort to express what they feel. Men often see a woman's jealousy as the root of all evil, forgetting that it's not always as irrational as it may appear and sometimes proceeds from a real failure on a man's part.

When we consider the stress of raising a family today, it's understandable that the imperious necessity of just making a living leaves little time and energy for couples to care for each other's emotional lives. Besides, some misunderstandings, although annoying, are not all that momentous; for instance, a husband who complains that his wife is trying to change him, or a wife who reproaches her husband for failing to listen to her. The conflicts that occur can be immense. There are wives who never cease correcting their husbands and who force them to appear a certain way in public (convinced that if they don't adhere to certain rules, they'll be misfits). And there are husbands incapable of listening attentively to their wives. At any rate, all indicators point to how "men ought to remember that women talk about problems to get close and not necessarily to get solutions. So many times a woman just wants to share her feelings about her day and her husband, thinking he is helping, interrupts her by offering a steady flow of solutions to her problems. He has no idea why she isn't pleased."[66]

She isn't pleased—although she doesn't say so, but just thinks it—because her husband, who doesn't seem to take any interest in the things she cares about, sees fit to subject her to a pedantic lecture on solutions she's already aware of. But she forgets how incomprehensible it is to him that she would

---

66. Gray, *Men are from Mars*, p. 41.

want to discuss a problem when she already knows the solution beforehand.

Other misunderstandings *are* substantial: especially those involving trust. In these cases the early, promising years can give way to nightmarish times. Tolstoy recounts such a case in one of his celebrated stories: "His wife began to be jealous without any cause, expected him to devote his whole attention to her, found fault with everything, and made coarse and ill-mannered scenes."[67] Everything depends on the climate of trust. If trust breaks down, everything falls apart. If trust is reestablished, things run smoothly. Author Gary Smalley recounts how, after six months of careful treatment, he managed to regain his wife's confidence. The acid test of this favorable climate between the two of them came when he asked her permission to go into seclusion for six weeks to write a book. She was perfectly willing—something very unusual compared to an earlier time, when any plan that didn't take her into account was sufficient grounds for a fight.[68]

Although it's a bit of a generalization, the following is a description of how a typical crisis is launched between a complicated wife and a more simpleminded husband. She's juggling professional work and her dedication to their children and the housework; he helps out a little at home, but his career is demanding. The ideal, of course, would be to combine, in each spouse, both simplicity and an openness to the complexities of life—goals to which both men and women ought to aspire. But the husband systematically neglects the details of affection, and his wife erroneously concludes that

67. L. Tolstoy, *The Death of Ivan Ilyich* (Whitefish, MT: Kessinger, 2004), p. 14.
68. See Gary Smalley, *If Only He Knew: What No Woman Can Resist* (Grand Rapids: Zondervan, 1996), p. 37.

he no longer loves her. She begins to fear that she's no longer first in his life and starts to look around for her presumptive "rival," which need not be another woman—it might be his relatives, friends, job, or hobbies. If she feels jealous, for example, because of how much time he dedicates to his career, she'll make hurtful remarks along these lines. Things would improve if she explained her hesitation to trust him, but she opts instead for a hostility that her husband, lacking empathy, neither expected nor understands. The storm is upon him, and he never saw it coming. To avoid it, it would have been enough for him to be more attentive to the nonverbal messages his wife has been trying to send him. Despite "the habitual feminine acquiescence to half-truths,"[69] one can often tell what a woman is thinking by reading her expression.

When there is empathy and understanding, though, one can always find an explanation even for what seems most irrational. Every time one spouse (assuming he or she is of sound mind) says or does something the other doesn't understand, the other spouse ought to realize there's something he or she isn't "getting" and seek the missing information, instead of assuming that the other has gone crazy or is acting out of malice. For instance, there's an explanation for the difficulty a woman sometimes has in saying simply to her husband, "You give the impression that I don't matter to you anymore."[70] A sensitive person, whose every hope is placed in love, suffers so terribly when she senses her chief source of self-esteem collapsing that she finds it very difficult to be sincere with the very person who is the source of her disappointment. Both spouses ought to be able to feel the harsh blow that one is

---

69. Gaite, *Irse de casa* (Barcelona: Anagrama, 1998), p. 93.
70. Gray, *Men are from Mars*, p. 65.

suffering, because they know how to put themselves in the other's place.

If this understanding is lacking, what began, perhaps, as a minor dispute about a work schedule will go from bad to worse. If husband and wife don't know how to put themselves in each other's shoes, both will feel unjustly treated. Both may think themselves unloved; both may believe that the other doesn't value their efforts to raise the family—efforts inevitably shared by husband and wife. Both feel aggrieved, and, unless they're humble, each will believe that only his or her view is correct. The reality is that they're each partly right and partly wrong. He has neglected the details of affection if, for example, breakfast and evening become times for merely reading the paper or watching the game on TV, leaving no room for any possible conversation. She, meanwhile, has forgotten that everyone needs times of recreation to "decompress" from the stresses of a demanding workday and prepare oneself for the next one. If they insist on talking past each other, misunderstandings will only pile up. He won't know how to read between the lines and will expound with cerebral arguments upon the reasons for his aggravation. She will see that he's misinterpreting her messages, and her conviction that her love is unrequited will be reinforced. They both mistake misunderstanding for a lack of love, neglecting the intuitions and subtleties so necessary for getting along.

It's complicated to redirect a situation gone bad. An ounce of prevention—detecting early on that trust is beginning to weaken—is worth a pound of cure. When one knows beforehand what is liable to happen and fights against routine, it's easier to spot the signs. One thermometer of feminine trust in a man's love is her openness to affection. A husband can sense his wife's lack of confidence in him when she is resistant to any kind of physical intimacy. Women, unlike some men, don't tend to separate love from sex.[71] If she doesn't feel loved, it's as if her body is blocked. Early on, when trust was still intact, any little gesture of love was met with an embrace. If, as the years pass, a husband notices that his wife won't even allow him to hold her hand, he should recognize the nonverbal message that her confidence in him has deteriorated.

Once the crisis has developed into a chronic condition, ample understanding and humility will be needed to heal it, in order to forgive each other and acknowledge one's own mistakes. "The cause of all evils and disturbances lies in nobody wishing to accuse himself."[72] It's possible to turn the situation around if both spouses understand that, after all, they still love each other. "Those who argue with each other desire each other" goes the saying (of course, this is not always the case). Some argue *because* they love each other: if they were indifferent, their arguments wouldn't last long. It's precisely because they care for each other that they each have a great power to wound. The path towards renewed harmony is tortuous if they focus on the scars that pride and accumulated wounds leave behind, but it is possible with forgiveness and mutual acknowledgment of love.

Indifference is the final stage in a relationship's deterioration. If no cure is found for routine misunderstandings, a moment will come when all affective resonance has vanished, at least on the part of one spouse. Evelyn Waugh describes it this way in one of his novels:

---

71. Women are right to refuse to separate the two: It would be to enter into a utilitarian dynamic unworthy of real love, more appropriate to prostitution. With this in mind, we can better understand the morality of the Catholic Church.

72. St. Dorothea, *Doctrinas*, Bk. 7.

I had played every scene in the domestic tragedy, had found the early tiffs become more frequent, tears less affecting, the reconciliations become less sweet, till they engendered a mood of aloofness and cool criticism, and the growing conviction that it was not myself but the loved one who was at fault. I caught the false notes in her voice and learned to listen for them apprehensively; I recognized the blank, resentful stare of incomprehension in her eyes, and the selfish, hard set of the corners of her mouth. . . . She was stripped of all enchantment now and I knew her for an uncongenial stranger to whom I had bound myself indissolubly in a moment of folly.[73]

Observe that the protagonist in this novel thinks that only the woman is blameworthy. This is very common. It's one of the reasons why it is so complicated, delicate, and risky to assess the *moral responsibility* in a broken marriage. Numerous factors are in play, delicate because proximity impedes impartiality, and risky because we will always lack some of the data; we would be unjust not to reserve definitive judgment to God. In any case, faced with such an unfortunate *denouement*, it seems inevitable to want to examine the facts. Even if only for the sake of understanding and profiting from the experience, it's wise to ask what went wrong, how it could have been avoided, and whether it is morally right for two people in the midst of conflict to definitively break a bond freely assumed that was meant to unite them for life. We have seen that marriage crises originate when real love and communication break down. To learn how to avoid this and determine whether the severance of the conjugal bond is ethically

---

73. E. Waugh, *Brideshead Revisited* (New York: Knopf, 1973), pp. 5–6.

acceptable, we must take one more step in our analysis. I will therefore consider the three indispensable elements necessary for making progress in love: desire, knowledge, and capacity. This simple outline offers the tools necessary to address the delicate questions that have arisen.

DESIRE, KNOWLEDGE, AND CAPACITY

To crown any moral endeavor with success, we have at our disposal three supports: *desire* (good will), *knowing* (an appropriate formation), and *capacity* (ability). Willpower is not sufficient; we also need desire, a whole compendium of knowledge, and a certain capacity, related to mental health, without which this ideal would remain inaccessible. Inversely, this same outline allows us to identify the three possible causes of moral evil: *ill will*, *ignorance*, and *incapacity*. The best of ideals can break down for want of will, formation, or capacity. In practice, these three tend to appear intermingled; the situation is seldom black and white. This is why it is so difficult to mete out moral responsibility with respect to concrete cases. However, with broad strokes we can affirm that evil use of the will is culpable, incapacity is not, and ignorance may be one or the other, depending on whether it's invincible. In a marriage crisis, for instance, there's always an element of ignorance. It is a rare case indeed that springs entirely from incapacity or ill will.

To be capable of happiness after assuming an irrevocable commitment, one needs to deepen one's love by persevering, acquiring the necessary formation, and enjoying adequate mental health. (If this third element is lacking, one can't validly enter into a marriage in the first place.) There are indeed certain psychological pathologies that render it impossible to assume the essential duties of marriage, in which case the marriage contract would be null. But the matrimonial bond, validly contracted, is by its very nature indissoluble. To have everything in common and to establish and raise a family is a major undertaking, if only because of unpredictable future ups and downs, but it's one that nobody is obliged to take on. This is why it's an act of mutual trust and an exercise of freedom: The spouses commit to being husband and wife for life. Thus, speaking of "my ex-wife" or "my ex-husband" makes no more sense than saying "my ex-son" or "my ex-daughter." A marriage between two persons fit to assume the commitment can only fail through lack of will or ignorance—and both of these can be remedied. The spouses are committed to learning to love each other well. "To say, 'I don't love you anymore' is meaningless in an interpersonal relationship. But to say 'I will work day by day to love you' implies freedom and responsibility, personal maturity, and untiring community of life."[74] If one spouse abandons the effort, he or she is failing to keep a promise freely and solemnly made, and leaves the other, who has promised to keep his or her own part of the bargain, in a deplorable situation. Divorce is thus morally inadmissible. (The case of physical separation of the spouses is very different, and there are circumstances that make it advisable or even necessary.)

Anyone enduring a marriage crisis deserves the greatest compassion, but not if it means *masking* the immorality of breaking a commitment that was freely and validly undertaken. Besides, even apart from ethics, this rupture doesn't offer the best approach, since problems always have some solution— unless good will or sufficient self-esteem are lacking. But in

74. J. B. Torelló, *Psicología abierta*, 2nd edition (Madrid: Rialp, 2003), p. 258.

such painful circumstances, we tend to look for a quick way out. Instead of confronting the laborious task of turning the situation around, we prefer to believe, for example, that we have simply chosen the wrong person. We blame our spouse for the failure and don't take time to find the real cause. If the problem isn't resolved at its root, it's very possible that the same difficulties will arise in any new relationship we establish. Consider, for example, the man who married five times only to realize in his old age that he could have been happy with any one of his wives. In the end, he saw that his true problem stemmed from his own deficient capacity for love.

We do well to remember, too, that a marital rupture involves a certain *social responsibility*. The bad example of those who throw in the towel encourages others to do the same. In the end, a divorce mentality begins to spread like a plague, as we see in today's world. The media bombardment and the shallow thinking that insists on an irresponsible "right to happiness" make people believe that divorce is a lesser evil, and that the price children pay is minimal, or at least unavoidable. In the old days, society perhaps tolerated infidelity but didn't declare it a legal right. In the sixteenth century, with the aim of protecting both parties, laws prohibiting clandestine marriages were promulgated. Today we see an unprecedented juridical insecurity; the number of those affected by divorce has risen,[75] and the law, responding to this painful situation, has ceased to protect those who freely choose an indissoluble union. There are countries in which a marriage contract is the easiest kind to break. One need not even present proof

---

75. According to figures published in Spain in 2008, four out of five marriages end in divorce during the first fifteen years. In some cities, the number of divorces exceeds the number of weddings.

of any wrongdoing; it's enough that one party wants to leave. In many places, only the Church guarantees a lifelong commitment. To the extent that the idea of "trial marriage" gains ground in the popular mind, the number of invalid marriages increases due to the intent to resort to divorce if difficulties arise. The Western view has indeed changed since the mid-twentieth century, when early movies that presented divorce as an option caused scandal.[76]

In any event, we seek to offer solutions to people who are having difficulty persevering in marriage, not just pass judgment on them. These thoughts are also applicable to other commitments—a vocation, for example. One could accurately inform those in these unhappy situations that something is lacking in the intensity or the depth of their love, but it would be better to help them discover why they haven't succeeded in loving more or better. Perhaps they lack good will, but it's also possible that they've gotten in over their heads (incapacity) or are ignorant of the human and supernatural means available for overcoming the problem. In that case it would be unjust to fault them for a lack of effort. We've already seen that there are self-sacrificing people who don't radiate happiness because they've unconsciously taken a voluntaristic approach to their devotion. Instead of reproaching them for their sadness, it makes more sense to teach them to fall in love again and to cultivate humble self-esteem. Mercy should always prevail. "When judgment is too rigid," Max Jacobs said, "let it be corrected with indulgence and charity. This mixture of piety and justice is the heart of the Christian—that is to say the modest—talent."[77]

---

76. The first film was perhaps *The Best Years of Our Lives*, which won an Oscar for Best Movie in 1946.
77. M. Jacob, *Advice to a Young Poet* (Madrid: Rialp, 1975), p. 37.

3.

The Ideal Attitude Towards Oneself

It is clear from the previous chapter that pride endangers each and every quality of the ideal love. We've observed, first of all, that a poor relationship with oneself hampers purity of intention and interior freedom. We've also seen that pride damages respect for the beloved: low self-esteem strengthens possessiveness and compromises emotional detachment. Finally, the capacity for generous sacrifice is also weakened by pride. Since humble self-esteem has turned out to be so crucial—both in averting difficulties and making possible the joy of deep love—we will now address the ideal attitude towards oneself. To determine just what that is, we'll need to dispel certain misunderstandings about humility.

HUMILITY DOES NOT MEAN UNDERVALUING ONESELF

Humility is that virtue which ensures a positive and realistic attitude about oneself. The classic approach contrasts humility with pride, or arrogance. Arrogance leads us to exaggerate our own excellence, imagining ourselves to be superior. Whoever knows how to lower oneself, on the other hand, is humble (the word comes from the Latin *humus*, meaning "ground"). But lowering oneself—identifying one's rightful place— does not mean an unhealthy self-contempt. In that case, we would fight one defect by succumbing to another. Humility is united to the truth: It's not good for us to overvalue *or* undervalue ourselves.

Because humility is opposed to arrogance, some mistakenly think it wise to foster low self-esteem at all costs. This mistakes the true humility of self-knowledge for a poor self-concept. Something like this happened to Henri Nouwen. He recalls:

> For a long time, I considered low self-esteem to be some kind of virtue. I had been warned so often against pride and conceit that I came to consider it a good thing to deprecate myself. But now I realize that the real sin is to deny God's first love for me, to ignore my original goodness. Because without claiming that first love, and that original goodness for myself, I lose touch with my true self and embark on the destructive search among the wrong people and in the wrong places for what can only be found in the house of my Father.[1]

Since humility is an encounter with the truth, it is important to be formed in this virtue, especially for those with a tendency to undervalue themselves. Insisting that arrogance is the sole danger for an insecure person could potentially rob him of the only self-esteem he has; instead, the chief goal ought to be learning to know, love, and accept oneself as one

1. Nouwen, *The Return of the Prodigal Son* (New York: Image Books, 1992), p. 107.

is. It's like pointing out to a shy person that he's blushing. Wouldn't it be more effective to help him learn to ignore it? He will then be able to open himself more to others instead of retreating into his shell, eliminating all prospects of love. Insistence on humility, understood merely as modesty, can lead to dejection. True humility forecloses anxiety and fear, which threaten the person who can't accept his limitations and ends up suffering from a complex if his value is questioned. Of course, if we follow Christ's example and teaching (see Lk 14:7–11), we will gladly choose a place beneath our rightful one, without thereby losing sight of our dignity. We're not meant to relinquish our rights out of cowardice or feelings of inferiority. On the contrary: we place ourselves at the service of others freely, forgetting our self-worth, gladly abandoning it into God's hands. Thus, humility entails a good relationship with oneself, which forestalls exaggerating both our virtues and our defects. It also keeps us from projecting both onto others, helping to prevent conceit and false modesty. "A person may be proud without being vain," points out Mary, a character in Jane Austen's *Pride and Prejudice*. "Pride relates more to our opinions of ourselves, vanity to what we would have others think of us."[2] To be humble is much more than behaving humbly; it is a deep-rooted attitude.

If we mistakenly believe that humility is the habit of undervaluing oneself, we risk disguising as virtue something born of pride. The pride hidden beneath false modesty may be even more corrosive than conceit. Georges Bernanos captures this in his play, *Dialogues of the Carmelites*. One of the young sisters is suddenly seized by the desire to hide, to disappear, so as to advance in humility. "I ask nothing more than

---

2. Jane Austen, *Pride and Prejudice* (New York: Charles Scribner's Sons, 1918), p. 18.

to pass unnoticed," she tells her prioress. Here is the response, charged with wisdom, about what may lie hidden beneath the girl's aspiration:

> Ah! That comes only with time, and wishing for it too vehemently does not help. . . . Oh, yes! You desire fervently to be in the last place. Distrust this desire, too, daughter. . . . Whoever wishes to lower herself too much runs the danger of overstepping the mark. For in humility, as in anything else, lack of moderation breeds pride, and that pride is much more insidious and perilous than the worldly sort, which often doesn't get beyond vainglory.[3]

HUMILITY IS THE TRUTH BETWEEN THE EXTREMES

Years ago, I read a book by Mark Kinzer, a Jewish convert to Christianity.[4] Describing the ravings of a fellow convert, he reveals one misguided interpretation of St. Paul's advice to count others better than oneself (see Phil 2:3). Taking out of context the apostle's advice to cultivate a spirit of service, the convert concluded that he should view everyone as superior to him. This idea, which he applied every time he met someone, became an obsession, and the result couldn't have been more deplorable. First of all, it was implausible: he ran into plenty of people who, from an objective point of view, didn't seem to be any better. In the end, he realized "never had he

---

3. G. Bernanos, *Diálogos de Carmelitas* (*Dialogues of the Carmelites*) (Barcelona: Plaza y Janés, 1976), p. 31.

4. See Mark Kinzer, *The Self-Image of a Christian: Humility and Self-Esteem*.

spent so much time thinking about himself and comparing himself with others."[5] Humility is the art of valuing and seeing ourselves as we are, without reserve, and accepting our strengths and our limitations. But pride is like the funhouse mirror that distorts reality, making us think we're worth more or less than we really are, which then translates into a dishonest relationship with others. Humble people live in harmony with themselves and those around them, conscious of a dignity of which nothing and no one can rob them. While they do strive to improve, they love themselves as they are, and they permit others to correct and judge them. The proud, on the other hand, live in a continual state of internal conflict that hampers their relationships with others. The manifestations of this sad state are innumerable, ranging from an excessive need to be the center of attention to a morbid desire to impress.

Some individuals seem full of self-confidence but are trembling inwardly just as much as others who scarcely dare to raise their voice. The pride that makes some people braggarts provokes in others a sickly restraint and fear of ridicule. The tendency to opposite extremes is common in our fragile nature. Think, for example, of the way various drunks behave. One might imagine oneself a hero; another might sink into dejection.[6] Bipolar disorder, a mental illness so prevalent today, is marked by periods of euphoria alternating with periods of depression. Healthy people also suffer fluctuations in their state of mind. Who hasn't had days of waking up ready to tackle the world and others

---

5. Kinzer, *The Self-Image of a Christian*, pp. 15–16.
6. St. Paul counsels judging oneself with sobriety (see Rom 12:3). Note that "sober" is the opposite of "drunk."

when everything is an uphill battle? But all of this has little to do with the exercise of freedom. On the moral plane, all of us—to a greater or lesser degree—have difficulty judging ourselves accurately. The interplay of extremes leads us to distinguish two types of pride: *vanity* and *self-rejection*. Both conceal the same lack of humble self-esteem; both are actually two sides of the same coin.

With great sincerity, Mark Kinzer recounts:

> I never thought this business of self-rejection was my problem. If I had one, my difficulties and defects went in the other direction: overconfidence, self-assurance, and arrogance. I always got very good marks in school and never lacked for good friends. I expressed my opinions clearly and I happily accepted the challenge of a good argument. In my work, I was a perfectionist: If Mark Kinzer did it, it was sure to be done right. I also harbored grand ambitions for my future. . . . Everything seemed within my reach. When I became a Christian, it seemed obvious to me that I'd need to renounce my previous conceit, perfectionism, and ambition. For years I struggled against those tendencies, repenting again and again. Finally, a more experienced Christian, and a profoundly wise man, told me that my problem was perhaps something more than a simple question of ambition and conceit. He ended by telling me, "I think you suffer from lack of self-confidence and an excessive desire for approval and security." I froze. Was it possible to attribute my energetic anxiousness to enjoy an excellent position partly to a desire for self-affirmation? Thinking about my life, I realized that indeed, this was so. I needed not only to repent of my

ambitiousness, but also to grow in my awareness of being a child of God who didn't need to affirm himself before his Father.[7]

SELF-FORGETFULNESS AND SELF-DECEPTIONS

In practice, the touchstone of humility is that spontaneous *self-forgetfulness* that results in a disinterested surrender to others. It's not a matter of claiming to be worthless or of stubbornly defending one's value. It's simply not bothering about esteem one way or another.

A misunderstanding of humility can sometimes make self-forgetfulness difficult. This happens, of course, when someone tries to force himself to think he's worthless, believing that this is his duty as a humble person. In fact, he never ceases revolving around himself in a continual gesture of scorn. The same thing happens with conceit.

Ordinarily, when faced with a lie, one's intelligence protests. But if self-deception becomes habitual, any error may be accepted. As the saying goes, "If you don't live according to what you believe, you begin to believe according to how you live." The root of this gradual moral deterioration is usually insincerity with oneself and a movement away from God. "Man begins by questioning the law of God in his conscience and ends without law, without God, and without conscience."[8] It's striking how those who go to confession frequently usually know what sins to confess, but those who go infrequently or not at all can't think of what to say.

---

7. Kinzer, *The Self-Image of a Christian*, pp. 18–19.
8. Urbano, *La madre*, p. 38.

Self-deception can advance quite far, as seen in the following quote from a witness to the horrors of the concentration camps.

> Outside of the prisons many of the state guards would show great self-confidence, making statements like, "I've never harmed anyone in my life; perhaps I may have failed to help someone out of carelessness." It almost sounds sarcastic, but it was typical among the most sadistic ones.[9]

Those who practice habitual self-deception end up believing their own lies; one's whole life can end up an extraordinary mythological fantasy. "The man who lies to himself and listens to his own lie comes to such a pass that he cannot distinguish the truth within him, or around him, and so loses all respect for himself and for others."[10] This is the sad moral deterioration to which pride leads. Lewis reveals this starkly in one of his books,[11] in which he identifies hell with supreme self-deception. Pride brings hell's inhabitants to such self-ignorance that nothing remains of their true "I." At the end of their lives, they are totally divorced from reality: all that is left to them is a false self. But while life lasts, if the conscience keeps whispering that self-deception is occurring, there's still hope of salvation: something still remains of the real "I."

In the drama of self-deception, the first thing to go is the conscience, followed by the understanding. An eloquent

---

9. I. Socías, *Sin miedo a la verdad: Conversaciones con Silvester Krcméry* (Madrid: Palabra, 1999), p. 144.

10. Fyodor Dostoyevsky, *The Brothers Karamazov* (New York: Macmillan, 1922), p. 40.

11. See Lewis, *The Great Divorce*, in *The Complete C.S. Lewis*: Signature Classics (San Francisco: HarperSanFrancisco, 2002).

passage from a play by Jacinto Benavente serves to illustrate this. When the shrewd Crispin proposes a deception for the sake of love to the good Leandro, he replies, "I cannot deceive myself, Crispin. I'm not one of those men who, having sold his conscience, thinks he must sell his reason, too." Crispin, very much in tune with reality, answers:

> That's why I told you you'd never be any good in politics. And you are right. The understanding is the awareness of the truth, and he who loses it among the lies of life is as if he had lost himself, for he will never again meet or recognize himself, and he himself will come to be just one more lie.[12]

HUMILITY AND PERSONALITY

A right understanding of Christian humility is crucial to the balanced development of the personality. It guards against self-deception and fosters inner peace and self-forgetfulness. It's a source of maturity and inner freedom. It enriches personal identity. However, a simplistic or erroneous vision of this virtue can lead to viewing it as something hostile to the distinctive traits that shape our own personal "style." Jesus Christ asks us to deny ourselves, but this dying to self, rightly understood, implies no loss of personality. On the contrary, the Christian finds himself in God because he knows God loves him just as he is. The humble self-esteem that allows him to die to self—in the sense of dying to his pride—is rooted precisely in this conviction. And the awareness of his

---

12. J. Benavente, *Los intereses creados* (Madrid: Biblioteca Básica Salvat, 1970), p. 109.

dignity enables him to offer himself to others with immense inner freedom. Indeed, God's love liberates us from our personal problems so that we're fit to devote our energy to others. In the words of Juan Bautista Torelló:

> Divine intervention into historical existence causes the *theia mania*, or divine madness, to arise, the "being outside of oneself" proper to truly great men, which is not loss of personal identity but that identity's expansion, almost to infinity, bringing it to fulfillment.[13]

We discover our true "I" by offering it to a "thou." "For where I am thine, I am wholly mine," goes one of Michelangelo's sonnets to Vittoria Colonna.[14] The ideal lover forgets himself in order to contribute to the happiness of the beloved. From this perspective we can see the true meaning of "dying to self." It's a question of burying the ego to surrender the self: to sacrifice (immolate) it, but not to commit suicide. As Thibon observes:

> Psychologically and metaphysically, immolation is the diametric opposite of suicide. To immolate myself is not to leap beyond life, but beyond *my* life with all that is limited and narrow in it. The supreme sacrifice can only be conceived of as breaking through a boundary, an absolute openness: not the death of the "I" but its total transmutation through love. . . .[15]

A free and loving surrender, then, requires healthy doses of humble self-esteem, fortitude, and magnanimity. Here the

---

13. G. Torelló, *Pazzo d'amore* in Studi Cattolici, VII-VIII, 1993, p. 421.
14. In G. von Le Fort, *La mujer eterna* (Madrid: Rialp, 1965), p. 88.
15. Thibon, *La crisis moderna del amor*, p. 48.

human and the divine are joined. God's love, together with our own efforts, makes this most remarkable gesture possible. Whoever, by God's grace, *loses* his life for love will *gain* it, both in this life—for he attains his true end: self-fulfillment through love—and also in the next (see Lk 9:23–25). "You will possess your souls," Christ promised those who would be faithful to him and deny themselves out of love (see Mk 8:34–37).

The importance of "being yourself," which we hear so much about these days, doesn't contradict the Christian ideal. God is the first one who desires that we not betray our own identity—in fact, he is the one who makes it possible. Certain atheist writers have contended that Christianity promotes depersonalization. They would be right if the Christian maxim of self-denial were interpreted as an invitation to betray oneself, or to cultivate servility without interior freedom. But, in fact, Christianity is an inexhaustible source of greatness of spirit—and of freedom, too. If it's not experienced this way, it's because the Christian message has been imparted wrongly or misunderstood. St. Josemaría writes:

> I am enchanted by evangelical humility. But what infuriates me is the timid, sheepish and irresponsible way by which some Christians discredit the Church. That atheist author must have had them in mind when he wrote that Christian morality is the morality of slaves.[16]

That "atheist author" (perhaps Nietzsche) couldn't see how to reconcile freedom and surrender. Fear of losing legitimate autonomy leads many people to assert their own independence at the expense of a loving dependence. They're

---

16. Escrivá, *Furrow*, no. 267.

"free"—but they don't love anybody. As St. Josemaría concludes: "In fact we are servants: servants raised to the rank of children of God, who do not wish to behave as if enslaved by their passions."[17]

No one subjected to an alien will is as free as the true Christian. Someone of exemplary life wrote the following affirmation, which, though subject to misinterpretation, synthesizes the liberty of the children of God: "At bottom, I never lowered myself, except before God and in His name. As long as I am contemplating God, my 'I' does not exist, but I abdicate before no one else."[18] This illustrates how Christianity synthesizes humility and healthy self-confidence. In the end, what's dangerous is not having a strong personality but being deluded into the self-sufficiency of thinking that one needs no one, not even God.

TWO ATTITUDES TOWARD ONESELF AND OTHERS

To sum up: We have seen that the ideal attitude towards oneself rules out self-deception. It fortifies personality, self-forgetfulness, and inner peace. We have referred to this realistic and positive attitude as "humble self-esteem." The term "pride" denotes its opposite. Now, in order to investigate the relationship between the love we receive, the love we possess, and the love we give, we'll introduce two new terms found in classical thought: 1) rightly ordered self-love and 2) *amor propio* (selfish love of self).

---

17. Escriva, *Furrow*, no. 267.
18. In H. Caffarel, *Camille C. ou l'emprise de Dieu* (Troussures: Feu nouveau, 1982), p. 321.

Ancient thinkers discussed these questions, although in different terms. St. Augustine, for instance, asks, "If you don't know how to love yourself, how will you be able to love your neighbor in truth?"[19] Love of oneself is a gauge for measuring the relationship between the love we receive and the love we give. The more and better the love we receive, the more and better is our love for ourselves and others. On the other hand, when the love we receive diminishes, difficulties with oneself and conflicts with others grow more likely.

We must first define rightly ordered self-love, distinguishing it from its polar opposite, *amor propio*. Philosophy and theology have both dealt with this question.

> Philosophical tradition has taught that there exists in every man a *natural* love of himself, an urge that can be neither evaded nor renounced, to preserve his own being and to unfold it towards its perfection until it attains its apogee: a yearning, in other words, to be happy.[20]

St. Thomas Aquinas explains the appropriateness of human persons loving their own good: they are made by nature to love all good, including their own. The love for one's own good orients one's life until death—although we must not forget that we are enriched and perfected through love for others. For this reason, Aquinas affirms that the love one feels for another "proceeds from the love that one feels for one's own person."[21] Love is the ideal framework for unfolding

---

19. Augustine of Hippo, *Essential Sermons* (New York: New City Press, 2007), Sermon 368, p. 415.

20. T. Melendo, *Ocho lecciones sobre el amor humano* (Madrid: Rialp, 2002), 4th ed., p. 175.

21. Aquinas, *Summa theologiae*, III, q. 28, a. 1, ad 6.

a person's potential, including the infectious desire to be happy by making others happy. All this presupposes that we're speaking of a *rightly ordered love* for oneself, in accord with the truth of the good and the hierarchy of goods.[22] Not loving oneself rightly, therefore, means distancing oneself from what essentially makes for happiness, mistaking it for transient enticements: alcohol, hedonism, ambition for power, drugs, or selfishness. The correlation between love for oneself and love for others is clear.

Theology also has addressed love of oneself from the perspective of charity. The reality of God's love for his creatures implies that those creatures should also love themselves. The Christian precept of "loving your neighbor as yourself" (Mk 12:31) forms the framework of this intimate relation between charity towards others and charity towards oneself. As the popular maxim says, "Charity begins at home." St. Thomas takes it a step further, arguing that in perfect love "one loves another in the same manner in which he loves himself."[23]

The proper love of oneself translates into a feeling of personal harmony, without narcissism, vanity, or envy—which are all manifestations of the polar opposite, *amor propio*, or pride. Luchin, a minor character in *Crime and Punishment*, is a good illustration of "that self-confidence that should rather be called *amor propio*." Dostoyevsky portrays him like

---

22. Aquinas, I, q. 60, a. 5; II-II, q. 19, a. 6.

23. Aquinas, *De spe*, a. 3, c. fine. The relationship with oneself is the model according to which we ought to orient the relationship with others, given that the former is *unity*, whereas the latter expresses only *union of affections*, and "unity is more noble than union" (Aquinas, *Summa theologiae*, II-II, q. 26, a. 4). This union is an inaccessible model for the union of love between creatures. Indeed, only the three Divine Persons are joined so as to constitute a perfect unity.

this: "Having come out of nothing, he loved himself morbidly, had a great esteem for his own talents and abilities, and even sometimes fell in love with his own face in the looking-glass."[24] These contrary attitudes are *inversely proportionate: amor propio* recedes when a healthy love of oneself is on the rise; inversely, *amor propio* increases as the relationship with oneself deteriorates. On the one hand, as one grows in awareness of one's own dignity, inner peace increases and the dissatisfactions generated by *amor propio* decrease. On the other hand, when *amor propio* is on the rise, there is a deficient self-esteem. In practice, given that we are already affected by egotism at birth, it's a question of progressively seeking to offset it by a growing consciousness of one's own dignity. This is a difficult and long-term project.

The interrelation between a rightly ordered self-love and *amor propio* helps us understand why egotism proceeds from ill will and a negative attitude towards oneself, which, in turn, generates all sorts of friction with others. The egotist loves himself or herself not too much, but too little and poorly. "The worst thing about egotists is that they don't love themselves in the least . . . and that's why they're unable to love others, because you can't draw out what's not there."[25] We can't give what we don't have. Those who don't know how to be kindly and gracious toward themselves will have difficulty being that way with others. Just as failure to accept one's own defects leads to intolerance for others' faults, it is when we're least patient with our own limitations that we're most critical of others. A humble and patient approach to our own weaknesses, though, facilitates understanding of others.

---

24. Dostoyevsky, *Crimen y castigo* (Barcelona: Planeta, 1982), p. 283.
25. Gaite, *Nubosidad*, p. 348.

These reflections may be useful for examining our own anxieties. For example, if someone rubs us the wrong way or irritates us, it may be simply because we're tired—but if we go deeper, with courage and sincerity, into self-knowledge, we may sometimes discover more dubious motives. If somebody seems annoying, it is perhaps, first, that we envy him for a virtue we lack; or second, that we share with him a defect which our pride makes it difficult for us to acknowledge; or third, because we've overcome this defect and think he ought to do the same. This may explain, for instance, the animosity, and even hostility, in couples with more than one child, toward the one who most clearly embodies a parent's defects—or toward the smoker who has no intention of giving up his addiction. To accept the truth humbly, despite any attendant pain, is vital for resolving the conflict.

PRIDE PUTS MENTAL HEALTH AT RISK

Our attitude towards ourselves is key to our happiness. Humble self-esteem lays the foundation for inner peace, and for an openhearted, generous dedication to the joy of others. On the other hand, if our dominant note is pride, inner tensions mount, compromising our psychological health and fostering conflict with others.

On analyzing the "pros" and "cons" of the heart, we've dwelt primarily on the will—on detachment and the possessive urge—in order to focus especially on the quality of love. Now we'll confront the serious mental problems that "losing one's head" involves, focusing more upon the intelligence, whose extremes are *lucidity* and *irrationality*. Still, given that the person forms a single whole, I prefer to use the term "susceptibility," since it relates as much to irrationality as to possessiveness.

Susceptibility, or "touchiness," is a typical mark of pride. It emerges, in the most extreme cases, before one's worth has even been called into question by another person's critical word or attitude. This doesn't occur in one who is aware of one's own dignity. But for those who suffer from "a disordered desire to be loved,"[26] this oversensitivity can even cloud the intelligence. It is manifest primarily in the imperious need for affirmation, followed by a systematic reaction of defensiveness to any criticism, and finally by resentment. Once pride is wounded, "they no longer desire to consult the intellect to determine whether they truly have been treated uncharitably. The fact that they *feel* offended appears to them sufficient."[27]

Such people seem destined to extremes that will end in a *disorder* or in isolation. They sometimes behave hysterically, like a child trying to be the center of attention, and it is not unusual for them "to fake pain, sadness, or illness to attract attention so that others will make a fuss of [them]."[28] Any inducement is sufficient for them to cry out for love and compassion, to "surprise us and disquiet us with their extraordinary acts, with their whims and extravagance . . ."[29] At other times, faced with fear of rejection and disappointment, their sensitivity leads them to be as discreet as possible, by isolating themselves or cultivating an unhealthy reserve. At either extreme, the oversensitive person is destined for a dead end: hysteria provokes rejection, and aloneness may ensure survival, but it's at the expense of all love, and thus all happiness. In the words of John Steinbeck, without love, a "[man's]

---

26. Von Hildebrand, *The Heart*, p. 129.
27. Von Hildebrand, *The Heart*, p. 131.
28. Escrivá, *Friends of God*, no. 131.
29. Dostoyevsky, *Humiliated and Insulted* (Barcelona: Juventud, 1985), pp. 292–293.

insides shrivel and his chest feels like a dry [wood] chip."[30] Still, if forced to choose between evils, *the conceit of isolating oneself* is even worse than *the vanity of calling attention to oneself*: it is better to love poorly than not at all.

In extreme cases, solutions are not easy—chiefly because we are perhaps faced with not simply a moral problem but some type of *neurotic pathology*.[31] A doctor's assistance may be necessary—although not as a substitute for any suitable spiritual assistance. Apart from this specialized attention, how can those who live with such people, or are responsible for their education, help them? It's not an easy answer; we must combine the most exquisite *understanding* with the most loving *demands*. Those with an insatiable thirst for appreciation need our compassion. Only those who have experienced such disorders understand the suffering they entail. But such compassion doesn't exclude being demanding. If it did, such people would remain trapped in a vicious circle of self-pity and irascibility, entrenched in a decimated and hopeless self.

Even apart from such cases, we all have our limits as to how much psychological weight we can bear. An extra ounce can leave us unbalanced. According to mental health experts, we're like fuel-powered vehicles. Each car has a larger or smaller gas tank. The art of preserving mental balance consists of learning to get optimal mileage from the available fuel. To avoid running on empty, we need to keep an eye on the fuel gauge, aware that stress is what consumes the supply the fastest. We "fill up" each time we enjoy ourselves and relax, when we get enough sleep and "disconnect" from whatever

---

30. John Steinbeck, *The Moon is Down* (New York: Penguin, 1970) p. 77.
31. We set aside endogenous depression and psychotic disorders for the purposes of this discussion.

is overwhelming us. At all costs, we must avoid depleting our reserves, as this can endanger our mental health. Those with a tendency to neurosis need to optimize their "fuel management," since they have a smaller—and also a leakier—"tank." To close off possible outflow, such people need to solidify their inner peace by solving any problems that come from pride. It's no use to continually fill a leaking tank.

The number of neurotic disorders has increased in modern societies. Depression is currently the fifth most common illness, and it is expected to rise to second place by 2020. Among other causes are the mad rush of competition and the breakdown of the family. The individual and his or her inalienable personal dignity are scarcely valued at all. In the struggle for survival, only the strongest stay afloat. The "weakest"—those who know less, have less, or can do less—suffer the most.

Certainly these illnesses have also existed in other eras, although with less frequency. An event in the life of St. Teresa of Jesus serves to illustrate.[32] She had to go to Toledo to help a noble lady who, upon her husband's untimely death, had sunk into a most profound melancholy (as depression was called in those days). With no knowledge of psychology but possessing abundant common and supernatural sense, the holy woman of Avila cured her using a twofold approach. First, she fostered self-forgetfulness, bringing others' needs to her attention. She never asked her how she was feeling but kept her up to date on all the servants' troubles. Second, she spoke to her of Christ's passion, helping her to offer all her sorrows to ease his redemptive suffering.

---

32. See J. L. Olaizola, *Los amores de Teresa de Jesús* (Barcelona: Planeta, 1992), pp. 106–115.

Part Two

TOWARDS A DEFINITIVE SOLUTION

4.

Conversion to Love

So far, we've brought to light all sorts of difficulties: self-sufficiency, human respect, immaturity, egotistical love, possessiveness, voluntarism, marriage problems, self-deception, oversensitivity, insecurity, neurotic disorders. . . . The origin in every case (with all its variants and manifestations) is pride—the difficulty of somehow trying to integrate it into genuine self-esteem and fruitful relationships. We must find practical ways to get to the root of the problems, heal their inner source, and solve them. Upon this firm foundation, love, the chief source of happiness, will deepen, enriching our inner self and all that surrounds us.

To meet this challenge, willpower alone is insufficient. We must purify our heart and fill it with God's love. Fortunately, we have at our disposal the inestimable aid of grace. Exertion is crucial but insufficient. Pride is like diabetes: incurable but treatable. If the diabetic doesn't take care of himself, his organism will be gradually sabotaged: disorders of the circulatory system, the vision, and so on, will appear. But if he diets and takes his insulin as periodic blood tests indicate, he can live a normal life, and the illness will not diminish his health. Something similar happens with pride. It never vanishes altogether;

as the saying goes, it "dies half an hour after its owner does."
But it can be kept at bay with the appropriate therapy.

And what is that therapy? It consists of establishing a humble self-esteem within us, something that offers us profound peace and can be recovered every time it's lost.

THE ROOT OF THE PROBLEM

First of all, though, we must admit that pride concerns us personally. We all suffer to one degree or another from this evil and its consequences. Acknowledging this is half the battle. Furthermore, it's crucial to be aware that willpower is inadequate to combat the perverse effects of pride. We're all born with a certain sickness of soul that needs healing. This is why we so often experience that "I want to, and I can't"—which provokes more questions than answers about how we act and why, leaving us defenseless against our own weakness. We would like, for instance, not to feel resentment towards someone who's offended us, but we feel it just the same. We'd like to forget some long-forgiven grievance, but we can't manage it. Three elements that determine the moral status of an action can help us to understand this dilemma. At the origin of every moral evil there are always three possible intermingled causes: 1) ill will (not wanting); 2) ignorance (not knowing); and 3) incapacity (not being able). To attain genuine love, we have three corresponding supports available to us: 1) will (wanting); 2) formation (knowing); and 3) mental health and the grace of God (being able to).

One of these alone—good will—is insufficient. As one of John Bosco's biographers noted, speaking of one manifestation of pride: "Anger is the outer foam of that torrent that bubbles within us: conceit. There are those who manage to compress and hide it and those who allow it to spill out to their exterior. The important thing is to block the cascade at the source of the torrent and its foam."[1] To block this "cascade" where pride has its source, it's worth investigating its deepest causes. This involves shifting our foundations, ideas, and sentiments—just as to show a garden's full splendor, we must aerate the soil and uproot the weeds. It's impossible to uproot pride entirely, but we have at our disposal the means of all but permanently neutralizing it.

A tenacious struggle against pride, to be really effective, modifies attitudes at their root—what Stephen Covey calls "basic paradigms." These paradigms are like a pair of glasses that conditions our view of everything. We abandon the search for a superficial "fix" and get to the root of the problem. In other words, we don't limit ourselves to fighting against the external manifestations of our defects; we seek to change our underlying dispositions, too. "If we want to make relatively minor changes in our lives, we can perhaps appropriately focus on our attitudes and behaviors. But if we want to make significant, quantum changes, we need to work on our basic paradigms."[2]

The will may crush some of pride's manifestations quickly, but it can't control and fully heal our complex inner world, so brimming with needs and unconscious disorders. Besides, this "environment" tends to deteriorate as life goes on and sins and traumatic experiences accumulate. Only God's grace, with our cooperation, can heal the heart's wounds. "Create in me a clean heart, O God, and put a new and right spirit within me," prays David in his penitential psalm (Ps 51:10).

---

1. H. Waust, *Don Bosco y su tiempo* (Madrid: Palabra, 1987), p. 77.
2. Stephen Covey, *The 7 Habits of Highly Effective People* (New York: Free Press, 2004), p. 31.

The "significant, quantum changes" Covey mentions occur by way of the purification of heart King David prays for. The heart is the meeting point of body and soul: the merely somatic and the merely spiritual. This is why we become "beastialized" or "spiritualized," depending on our moral perfection. Becoming more spiritual does not mean dehumanization. On the contrary, it places our passions at the service of our spiritual powers, gradually consolidating the unity of our nature, which is at once animal and spiritual. We "make ourselves" or "unmake ourselves." Purification of heart implies a perfect integration of all our potencies, ordered to the central goal: to love more and more, better and better. This is the best path towards a fulfilled life. Nothing offers us so much happiness as a deep love: Our "I" only reaches fulfillment in offering itself freely and disinterestedly to a "thou."

To secure our wholeness, we must make good decisions, since virtue integrates and vice disintegrates. A virtuous life allows us to live in harmony with God, with ourselves, and with others. Cold indifference does just the opposite. In the words of Bl. John Paul II, "Sin alienates man from God, and alienates man from himself and from others."[3] Like it or not, our decisions foster or sabotage our inner growth. In the end, our human nature is like an instruction booklet that accompanies an appliance we purchase. It's the key to knowing what kind of being we are and how we ought to act. It would be a shame to waste our energy pursuing goals that won't develop us. "Some people work diligently for years on end to achieve something that in reality is destroying them as persons. It's tragic but extremely common."[4] The more closely we follow

---

3. John Paul II, *Dies Domini*, no. 63.
4. Llano, *La Vida Lograda*, p. 42.

the "instructions," the more integrated all our powers will be, and the better our chances of living a fulfilled life. By contrast, if we ignore our "instructions," we will witness a gradual degradation, if not a rupture, of the various elements united in us. Moreover, our sins sadden God as they degrade us as persons. As Javier Echevarría recalls:

> Sin is not a peripheral matter that leaves its subject unchanged. Precisely because it is an act against the truth about us—against what we truly are and what we are truly called to be—it affects us in the depth of our human nature, deforming it. Every sin wounds man, disturbing the balance between the dimensions of sense and spirit, and generates in the soul an intimate disorder between the various faculties: intelligence, will, affectivity.[5]

We must retrace sin's path, straightening out its twists and turns. This is a "penance" which, sooner or later, we all are required to perform. If we want to enter heaven, we'll have to purify our souls—here or in purgatory. We require a deep inner conversion, through the warmth of divine grace and the cooperation of our own good will. Awareness of God's love, in the end, is what most effectively cleanses our heart, procuring the humble self-esteem that thwarts our pride. Only in learning how to "empty ourselves" of ourselves will we be able to "fill ourselves" with God—and the more we do this, the easier it becomes to empty ourselves further. Here's how St. Augustine explains it:

> This is what the saints did: they despised external things. . . . They penetrated themselves and looked at

---

5. Echevarría, *Itinerarios de vida cristiana* (Barcelona: Planeta, 2001), p. 90.

themselves; they found themselves within themselves and were displeased; they ran to the one who could reform them and restore their lives, the one on whom they would fix their gaze, in whom their own works would perish and that which he had created in them would remain. This is denying oneself; this is loving oneself rightly.[6]

The way of purification is long and mysterious: long, because of the many disorders to repair and wounds to heal; mysterious, because the action of grace is subtle and its effects cannot be measured like empirical constants. When we undergo radiation therapy, we observe its effects, but we cannot perceive the rays. The collaboration between God's grace and personal freedom is equally mysterious. Every profound conversion contains its secrets. God can easily heal a bodily illness. But the illnesses of the soul, tied to an identity that God will always respect, are healed only with our cooperation. The cure tends to arrive in times of crisis, which are especially propitious for deep reflection. These are moments of complexity, when it becomes easier to shift the foundations of a person's whole life. Some grow angry with God, not realizing that, all too often, our wounds are the only doors to our souls that we leave open for him. Paradoxically, these critical moments can present the best chance for fulfillment—or just the opposite, depending on our inner disposition. If we understand how crucial divine aid is to the healing of our wounds, we can recover our appreciation of the Church's recommendation that we practice frequent confession, even in the absence of mortal sin. Receiving this sacrament is like getting an invisible radiation treatment. Sooner or later, the results will be evident.

---

6. Augustine, Sermon 330, 3–4.

A Dignifying and Healing Grace

Fortunately, we can count on grace to help us face the profound inner change that all these reflections propose. Christ's redemption procures for us a grace that can heal the effects of original sin and restore our dignity as God's children. This is one of the truths of the Faith on which Christian hope is founded.[7] It is the good news: The salvation that Christ offers us is the best medicine for our wretchedness and provides the chance to recover our full dignity. It opens up generous horizons, for now Christ's grace, by freeing us from slavery to pride and establishing our humble self-esteem, allows us access to the joy of profound love.

During the Last Supper, Jesus gave his disciples a "new commandment": to love one another as he loves (see Jn 13:34). This commandment contains a veiled promise that he will help us keep it. The commandment is "new," for one thing, because the depth of love it requires "is not possible for man by his own strength alone. He becomes *capable of this*

---

7. Since from now on we will be discussing truths of Faith, I will summarize their foundation for those readers who may be unfamiliar with the subject. Christian faith is founded on the divinity of Christ. If we believe him when he affirms his divinity (see Jn 8:24; 10:30; 14:7–11; Mt 26:64; Mk 14:62), his testimony is infallible. As Thomas Aquinas confesses in his beautiful and oft-sung Eucharistic hymn, *Adoro te Devote*, "I believe all that the Son of God has spoken; / There is nothing truer than this word of truth." Thus, the Christian faith is not founded on the experienced sentiments of those who are seeking God; it is he himself who has taken the initiative, revealing himself objectively (see 1 Jn 1:1). Analogously, "Christian hope is not an illusion but an anchor that ties us to heaven, where Christ has preceded us" (Pope Benedict XVI, homily of May 4, 2008). The Catholic faith possesses the maximum guarantee of truth. Christ, who, being God, always keeps his promises, assures the Church of a mysterious divine assistance that preserves it from error regarding truths taught definitively by the Magisterium (see Mt 16:18–19; Lk 10:16; Jn 21:15–17).

love only by virtue of a gift received."[8] Without the aid of grace, we wouldn't be able to imitate Christ.

This gift is called "sanctifying grace." God, who is love (see 1 Jn 4:8), reveals and communicates himself through Christ. The grace that heals us of our incapacity for profound love is the gift of the Holy Spirit, obtained by Christ on the cross. This supernatural gift transforms us from within[9] and enables us to love as Christ loves. To bring about this mysterious transformation, the Paraclete creates in us gradually three related effects: he *enlightens* our intellect to understand God's love, he *inflames* our will to ignite the desire to respond, and he *purifies* our heart to conform our affections more and more to the affections of Christ's own.

In Latin, *salus* has a double meaning: "salvation" and "health." To *save*, one must *heal*. The saints (those who, despite their defects, attain the perfection of love) are saved. For this to be possible, curative grace is required. Only God is holy; only he loves in a wholly perfect way. And it is Christ—God made man to save us—who, through sanctifying grace, elevates us to the dignity of children of God. He removes the dregs of egotism that sin has deposited in our nature. "Grace *heals and elevates*," theology affirms: It *heals* our incapacity to love well—freely, respectfully, detachedly, and disinterestedly—and it *elevates* us to the dignity of children of God. If our main illness is the pride that perverts our love, it's no wonder that one "treatment" grace uses is helping us to become aware of this elevation.

Christ is at once the *model* and *source* of perfect love. He teaches us and, with this dignifying and healing grace, enables

---

8. John Paul II, *Veritatis splendor*, no. 22.

9. See John Paul II, *Dominum et vivificantem*, no. 59 and *Redemptor hominis*, no. 18.

us to love as he does. Therefore, to the degree that we let grace penetrate us, we can reach that happiness that consists of giving and receiving a love of great profundity. Holiness, then, is possible. According to Church teaching, all the baptized are called to holiness.[10] And the example of innumerable saints, most of them anonymous and ordinary,[11] confirms that we can all reach this perfection of love, whatever our life circumstances. The unsuspected breadth of the holiness that our Redeemer's grace opens to us is vital because, accustomed to our faults, we tend to shrink our expectations, as if we could never aspire to more than a bogus little love. André Frossard tell us: "The great drama of the human species is our failure to understand love and our habit of fixing limits to it that exist nowhere except in our own hearts."[12]

Still, grace's indispensable role doesn't dilute the importance of the ascetical struggle necessary to acquire good habits and fight evil tendencies. All is grace, but God obtains that grace for us insofar as we predispose ourselves—with humility and good works—to receive it. Our will is like a muscle we train daily so that it will respond well when we need it. If our will is weak, it will disappoint us when the time comes to do good and avoid evil. At the same time, we need to collect "greedily" that grace that can heal our defects. Christ gives it to us primarily through the sacraments, especially the ones we can receive frequently: confession and the Eucharist.

---

10. The universal call to holiness, which St. Josemaría was already preaching in the 1930s, was proclaimed several decades later by the Second Vatican Council. "All the faithful of Christ of whatever rank or status, are called to the fullness of the Christian life and to the perfection of charity" (*Lumen gentium*, no. 40). See also *Catechism of the Catholic Church*, nos. 2012–2016.

11. The Church celebrates all these unknown saints liturgically on November 1st.

12. A. Frossard, *Preguntas sobre Dios*, 3rd edition (Madrid: Rialp, 1992), p. 93.

THE GREATEST DIGNITY

To support the action of that grace, we must examine our life, accept our limitations, and find our remedy in God's love. And I don't mean a merely generic love; each of us is everything to him. As Leo Trese puts it, "On this fruitful reality I must build my entire spiritual life."[13] The key to neutralizing pride's effects lies in understanding how to offset the reality of our wretchedness with the dignity of being children immensely loved by God—counterbalancing conceit with "the humble joy of knowing I am loved by God, not because I deserve it but because he is good, because he is all love. And I need to know I am loved personally, as someone unique, as *someone before God*. As a person, as someone exceptional."[14] Love is synonymous with devotion (*entrega*), and when the protagonist is God, we receive his unsearchable treasures. The divine filiation Christ has won for us entails a mysterious but real participation in his divinity. This is why Emmanuel Mounier affirms that, "among the faults of existing as a created being in God's image, called to increasing divinization, none is worse than this: the rejection of one's own dignity."[15]

The love of God confers an inestimable dignity, which dwarfs any concerns about our worth. These concerns come from without, or perhaps from our own insecurity. "The most important truth, which can procure for us a high level of self-respect and self-esteem, is the truth according to which God esteems us."[16] Thus, we can avoid anxiety about "what people will say." To exchange "human respect"

---

13. Leo Trese, *Dios necesita de ti*, 6th edition (Madrid: Palabra, 1990), p. 25.

14. Cardona, *Metafísica*, p. 130.

15. E. Mounier, *L'affrontement chrétien* (London: Harvill Press, 1955), p. 87.

16. Kinzer, *The Self-Image of a Christian*, p. 34.

for "divine respect," we need to *see ourselves and value ourselves as God does*. In this way, we give more weight to God's esteem and lose the fear of others' contempt. As Leo Trese says: "How sad that, knowing how much God loves me, I whine and lament because people don't love me as much as I wish! This is just as foolish as a multimillionaire complaining about losing a quarter in the slot machine."[17] A priest rendered quadriplegic in a car accident likewise concluded: "I believe an immense Love presides over my life. And over everyone's, though many people don't realize it. To sum up my problem, I'd say I'm like a multimillionaire who has only lost a few dollars."[18]

While appreciation of others fosters our self-esteem (we're only human), it would be deplorable for it to depend solely on our peers. The surest way to evaluate ourselves correctly is in the glance of the One who loves us most and best. Here we find the most reliable source of freedom and inner peace. Very instructive is something St. Josemaría would pray when he was the target of great calumny. "Lord, if You don't need my honor, what do I want it for?" A little later, he spoke of it himself, saying: "And it was hard; it was hard because I'm very proud, and I shed a few tears. . . . But ever since then, I couldn't care less about the whole thing!"[19] "That night," comments Pilar Urbano, "devoid of his own esteem . . . he crossed the threshold of genuine freedom."[20]

---

17. Trese, *Dios necesita de ti*, p. 22.

18. L. de Moya, *Sobre la marcha. Un tetrapléjico que ama la vida* (Madrid: Edibesa, 1997), p. 68.

19. Pilar Urbano, *El hombre de villa tevere* (Barcelona: Plaza & Janes, 1994), p.168.

20. Urbano, *La madre*, p. 337.

LOVE AND LOVES

God's love easily surpasses the best of all possible human loves. If we could truly fathom this, we'd be left breathless. Only he can give himself with no limitation whatever. One can only give as much as one possesses, and human beings do not possess themselves. We can offer something of ourselves—time, gifts, affection—but not our whole person. God, though, can give himself fully, since he doesn't consist of parts (being an infinitely simple substance), and he does possess himself fully. The result of this substantial self-giving is astonishing.

An intimate bond with Jesus Christ, the Incarnate Word, is formed whenever we receive the Eucharist. This bodily and spiritual fusion is the deepest of unions. He nourishes us with his own glorious flesh, something not even the best of mothers can do, and he gives himself to us in a manner so astonishing that it surpasses our intellect's abilities. "Take," he says, at the beginning of the consecration—"take me," in the singular—waiting humbly for each of us to freely accept his offering of love. It's a shame that our senses don't perceive these marvelous realities.

In order to fulfill our deepest longings, we all need the absolute, enduring, and unconditional love that only God can give. That is the answer to the question put by the protagonist of a novel who, in the midst of a personal crisis, asks his psychologist, "You mean this desire of mine to be loved, to be loved tenderly, passionately, and exclusively isn't ever going to be satisfied?"[21] St. Augustine condensed this same uneasiness in his celebrated exclamation, "You have made us, O Lord, for yourself, and our heart is restless until it rests in you." This is

---

21. A. J. Cronin, *The Spanish Gardener* (Madrid: Palabra, 1994), p. 105.

the best summary of a long search, begun in inner emptiness and ending in the conviction that only God can quench the thirst of the unsatisfied self. As Javier Echevarría recalls:

> The human being has an infinite capacity that only the Infinite, God himself, can satisfy. There is a depth within us that nothing and nobody, except God, can ever fill; therefore, there is—even in the greatest friendships and the greatest loves—a certain experience of confinement, of unconquered solitude.[22]

Other people's love can help us—after all, human love is gratifying and tangible, but it offers no lasting solution.

As Pope Benedict XVI affirmed at the beginning of his pontificate, "If we let Christ into our lives, we lose nothing, nothing, absolutely nothing of what makes life free, beautiful and great. . . . Only in this friendship is the great potential of human existence truly revealed."[23] Friendship with the Lord *purifies*, *harmonizes*, and *ennobles* all other loves.

We'll begin with its *purifying* aspect. We have seen how, in the love between man and woman, passionate love is meant to serve spiritual love. The ancient Greeks called the passion *eros* and friendship *philia*. Christians preferred the term *agape* (*caritas* in Latin), "which occurs rather infrequently in Greek usage" and "point[s] to something new and distinct about the Christian understanding of love."[24] In fact, we have here a third level of love's depth. The term "charity" (contrary to its condescending and disembodied meaning in some circles) appeals to a way of loving even an enemy with the affection

---

22. Echevarría, *Itinerarios de vida cristiana*, p. 132.
23. Benedict XVI, Homily of April 24, 2005, at the inauguration of his pontificate.
24. Benedict XVI, *Deus caritas est*, no. 3.

of *eros* and the respect of *philia*. This charitable love exceeds our own powers; it's a gift we receive from God. To establish an inexhaustible font of self-giving in the soul, the Holy Spirit enkindles the will, illuminates the intellect, and purifies the heart, easing the humble self-esteem that makes profound love possible.

The love of God also allows us to *harmonize* human loves. Family, friends, and professional work are all valuable sources of self-esteem, but they require a corrective element to ensure that they stay in their proper position. If God takes first place, self-image improves and detachment with both others and one's work becomes possible. By contrast, when God isn't the chief source of self-esteem, the dissatisfied self finds its relations with others deteriorating and begins to put work where it doesn't belong. Cut off from God's love, one finds that the need for affection gives rise to possessiveness regarding relatives and friends. Even professional success can be hampered by a lack of impartiality. One works no longer for love, but out of vain self-complacency.

Finally, God's love *ennobles* other loves. Every human love contains something divine. It's a pale but real reflection of divine love, like the moon that shines in the night because it reflects the sun. So, too, the opaque brilliance of our human loves ought to recall the splendor of God's love. Normally, though, love, "stripped of any absolute dimensions, captivates men as if it were the absolute. They allow themselves to be led by the thrill and do not seek to found their love on the Love that does possess an absolute dimension."[25] Thus, for

---

25. Karol Wojtyła, *El taller del Orfebre* (Buenos Aires: Ciudad Argentina, 1998), p. 114. This play by the future pope was published for the first time under a pseudonym in a Polish magazine in 1960.

someone who expects from the moon what only the sun can give, disappointment in love is inevitable. And if one persists in mistaking the moon for the sun, possessiveness grows, and love loses its glow. This is why Gustave Thibon says, "To love is to hunger together, not to devour each other."[26] If their love is to reflect the purity of eternal love, lovers must preserve a certain modesty. To pursue consummation at all costs renders love mortal. All this is reason enough to put God first, preventing any finite love from becoming the sole source of our self-esteem. It's not that we love others any *less* but that we love him *more*. Only thus can we love others *better*—with an emotional detachment that respects the independence of someone who is loved first and foremost by God. On the other hand, the fidelity of divine love contrasts with the uncertainties and insecurity of human love where, depending on the beloved's response, there is room for just three possibilities: *requited love, unrequited love,* and *impossible love.* When reciprocity is lacking, things are unpleasant, but at least the consolation of being able to offer the beloved something remains. In the third case, when the beloved does not even let him- or herself be loved, we can only continue in love and happiness if we love God *in* the beloved. Offering the Lord the pain of this rejection, we can give him happiness, and, through him, contribute to the good of the one who rejects our love.

What happens, though, when a fellow creature's love is the locus of our life's ultimate meaning? Disappointment is possible; happiness, at best, is probable; the future, uncertain. With human love, indifference and treachery may ensue, and the sorrow of absence after the beloved's death is inevitable.

---

26. Thibon, *Nuestra mirada ciega ante la luz* (Madrid: Rialp, 1973), p. 171.

The protagonist of a Sándor Márai novel expresses his unrest after his wife's death:

> There's patience, service to others, a whole world. . . . Still, you see, all of that is empty, mysteriously empty, if your interests aren't moved along any current. That strange current between one person and another. Life comes down to that. Of course, there are other things that make it possible to get through life. But the machinery just keeps running without any meaning, without being good for anything.[27]

A Susana Tamaro novel addresses similar themes. The heroine has the courage to confront an inner process that unfolds after the unexpected death of Ernesto, the man she loves most. She regains her self-confidence and discerns the true foundations on which her existence is built. The heroine recalls:

> After Ernesto's death, I was sunk in the deepest exhaustion. I had suddenly realized that the light I had shone with during the last few years didn't come from within me. It was just a reflected light. The happiness, the love, and the life that I had experienced didn't really belong to me, but had only worked like a mirror. Ernesto emanated light and I reflected it. Once he was gone, everything grew dark again.[28]

Instead of seeking refuge in a substitute for the departed, she opts for facing herself and accepting that the source of her unhappiness lies within her, in her own lack of self-esteem:

---

27. S. Márai, *Divorcio en Buda* (Barcelona: Salamandra, 2002), p. 172.
28. Tamaro, *Donde el corazón te lleve*, p. 156.

For a moment I thought of latching onto some new crutch. . . . That idea didn't last long. Almost immediately I realized that that would just be my umpteenth mistake. At forty, there's no room for mistakes. If you suddenly find yourself naked, you need to have the courage to look in the mirror and see yourself as you are. I had to start everything over from scratch.[29]

She sets out on a path of radical change to conquer her lost happiness. She realizes, first of all, that a good relationship with herself is the best foundation for rebuilding her existence. Then she discovers the love of God, which, by shoring up her self-esteem, allows her to dedicate herself disinterestedly to the happiness of others.

The fulfilled, successful life isn't at the mercy of circumstances beyond our control. Self-pity is fruitless, only making a difficult situation worse. We need to secure our happiness to a *habit*—that of profiting even from adversity. Good navigators learn from their mistakes. A sailor who flounders in a storm profits from the experience to ride out future storms more skillfully: he doesn't blame the climate. We can face misfortunes in the same way. If we notice that we are crushed when someone slanders us, we can make a point of becoming more independent of others' opinions; if we suffer a romantic disappointment, instead of lamenting our lot, we can review the sources of our self-esteem so that our happiness no longer depends solely on the love of a fellow creature.

In short, we will be truly happy only if we depend on God's love. Otherwise, we'll never experience that joy of which no one and nothing can rob us—as long as we preserve

---

29. Tamaro, *Donde el corazón te lleve*, p. 158.

our good will. The best happiness is independent of any eventuality. Many make their happiness contingent on future possibilities: They say to themselves, "No, I'm not quite satisfied yet, but once I get that diploma, or once my marriage situation is straightened out, or once my financial problems are solved, then I'll feel fulfilled." With this attitude, the longed-for happiness will never arrive. Instead of coveting transient successes, we ought to go straight to the source of our greatest dignity: the marvelous reality of being loved fully by God. Since our pride is ravenous for esteem, the best way to keep it in check is to offer it "food" that will satisfy it for good. Why place our hopes in an uncertain future when, right now, the Lord loves us as we are, in our present state, with whatever we do or don't possess? It would be a shame to spend our lives seeking a love we already have. If we're not happy here and now, we may never be.

CONFRONTING THE TRUTH ABOUT ONESELF

Inner conversion means no longer postponing a real examination of conscience, one that plumbs our innermost depths, neither avoiding uncomfortable questions nor living in fear of the answers. "Finding loopholes when you don't want to look inside yourself is the easiest thing in the world," affirms Tamaro's heroine. "There's always someone else to blame; you need a lot of courage to accept that the guilt, or, better, the responsibility, belongs to no one but you."[30]

We must acknowledge reality, the good and the bad, and then make the firm decision to adhere only to what really deserves our loyalty, changing course when necessary. Again

---

30. Tamaro, *Donde el corazón te lleve*, p. 163.

and again, in times of crisis or fair weather, we can reorient our life, abandoning ourselves to God's unconditional love.

Faced with our own defects, if we're ignorant of God's love or choose to disregard it, we have two options: acknowledging our faults and succumbing to depression, or deceiving ourselves and "surviving." Deception may be more pleasant than depression, but the lie interferes with our inner peace because our intelligence always protests. Christianity offers the best choice: *living to the full*, having recourse to the One who, overflowing with mercy, can free us from both depression and deception. Hence the importance of remaining open to the whole truth about ourselves so that we can enjoy this fullness of life with which God's love floods us.

Adjusting the course of our entire life is no simple matter. A mixture of insecurity and pride hampers us. If we've grown accustomed to leaning on false security, we may feel "dizzy" when we abandon it for the adventure of an interior revolution. It's as if we were stepping off the shifting sands that were keeping us afloat, in a panic at leaving them—or as if someone were inviting us to jump in the dark from a third-floor balcony to an invisible cushion held by firemen. We've functioned too long with one paradigm to change just because somebody offers an alternative. As long as no serious problems emerge, our model offers us a certain equilibrium and security. But even when troubles arise, some continue to cling to their old habits. Perhaps unconsciously, they allow their pride to keep them from facing the truth about themselves. If they have been hiding their weakness for years behind an iron shield, it's no wonder that, even when the depth of God's love is made clear to them, they may not be willing or able to alter their accustomed worldview. Some see things clearly only at the very end, like Ivan Ilyich, the Tolstoy character who only finds true peace when, in the moment of agony, he realizes that his whole conscious life has been one long deception.[31]

The antidote to self-deception is prayer—thus the importance of seeking within each day a prime moment to speak with God alone, remembering that though no one knows our weakness as he does, he loves us anyway, exactly as we are. He wants us to strive to conquer our defects, but his love doesn't depend on whether we succeed. Could we find a better interlocutor? Jesus Christ himself gave us an unforgettable example, in the Garden of Olives, of a trusting and sincere prayer to his father. Knowing that he will be judged and condemned that night, he exclaims, "Father, if thou art willing, remove this cup from me; nevertheless not my will, but thine, be done" (Lk 22:42). As André Sève notes:

> Never has Jesus been so close to us. Even to assuming the fear of what God might ask of a man. For us, by contrast, such fear leads us to avoid prayer. . . . Where could we learn, if not here, that praying is not playing at praying, but seizing from God whatever we need to accomplish what he expects of us?[32]

THE ELDER BROTHER

Inner conversion is more difficult for the Christian who is overconfident of his own virtue. Thus Christ reproaches the Pharisees in the Gospel with fulfilling every precept of the law meticulously, not for love of God but to feel superior. This

31. Tolstoy, *The Death of Ivan Ilyich & Other Stories*, 4th edition (Barnes and Noble Classics, 2003).

32. A Sève, *30 Minutes for God* (Paris: Le Centurion, 1974), p. 33.

overconfidence prevents them from understanding the merciful love he preaches. In this context, we turn to the parable of the prodigal son, which will deepen our understanding of the conversion to love that I've proposed as the solution to the difficulties of pride.

The story is familiar. The younger of two sons asks his father for his inheritance, which he uses to go his own way, alone. "He took his journey into a far country, and there he squandered his property in loose living" (Lk 15:13), the Gospel recounts. Having spent it all, after a time of need he decides to return home. His father, far from throwing his attitude in his face, celebrates with a feast. The elder brother's reaction is very different. He is vexed with his father, whom he reproaches with never having rewarded him for his years of service. For this reason, "he was angry and refused to come in" (Lk 15:28). Taken aback, his father explains his joy on the return of the younger one, which is not intended as an insult to his firstborn.

This parable, one of the most eloquent in all of Scripture, illustrates the Christian journey by way of two different routes. The younger brother's return portrays an initial conversion. But this fledgling gesture may remain unfinished as the years pass—as with the elder brother—if one fails to purify one's heart. Blinded by pride, instead of celebrating his little brother's return, the elder brother grows irritated and parades his own merits. The counterpoint between the two approaches is the father, who forgets about himself entirely and lives only for the happiness of his sons.

The three characters portrayed in the parable recall the "pagan-Jew-Christian" typology of St. Paul,[33] used to illustrate the true freedom Christ has won for us (see Gal 5:1).

---

33. See the first 11 chapters of the Epistle to the Romans, especially 1:18—3:31.

According to the apostle, there are two ways to corrupt true liberty: 1) the libertinism of the *pagan*, who becomes a slave of his passions (the first stage of the younger brother's story), and 2) the lack of interior freedom of the *Jew* who becomes a slave to the law (the older brother). The *Christian*, on the other hand, is enslaved neither to sin nor to the law. This is the father in the parable. The indolent pagan has to be reminded that, "when man wishes to free himself from the moral law and become independent of God, far from gaining his freedom, destroys it."[34] The righteous Jew should be congratulated for his fidelity to the law but shown that in order to go beyond moralism, one doesn't abolish the law but remains subject to it out of love (see Rom 3:31 and 6:15). "If the Son makes you free, you will be free indeed," says Jesus (Jn 8:36). "We relish our freedom of action," attests St. Josemaría "as a gift of God."[35] St. Paul experienced in his own life the difference between being a *Jew* and a *Christian*. As Pope Benedict XVI explains:

> Before his conversion Paul had not been a man distant from God and from his Law. . . . In the light of the encounter with Christ, however, he understood that with this he had sought to build up himself and his own justice, and that with all this justice he had lived for himself. He realized that a new approach to his life was absolutely essential.[36]

The elder brother resembles the Jew of the Pauline typology because although he fulfills the precepts of the law, his

---

34. Congregation for the Doctrine of the Faith, Instruction *Libertatis conscientia*, March 22, 1986, no. 19.

35. Escrivá, *Friends of God*, no. 35.

36. Discourse of General Audience, Nov. 8, 2006.

pride makes him egotistical. For this reason, when his father begs him to come to the feast in honor of the new arrival, he is full of resentment and replies, "Lo, these many years I have served you; and I never disobeyed your command; yet you never gave me a kid, that I might make merry with my friends. But when this son of yours came, who has devoured your living with harlots, you killed for him the fatted calf!" (Lk 15:29–30). He sets boundaries: "This son of yours," he says. He won't even acknowledge the "convert" as his brother. Pride makes him uncharitable and envious, and it hardens his heart against both his brother and his father.

This parable demonstrates two things: the runaway younger brother's necessary repentance and the elder's necessary conversion. As Nouwen notes:

> Not only did the younger son, who left home to look for freedom and happiness in a distant country get lost, but the one who stayed home also became a lost man. Exteriorly he did all the things a good son is supposed to do, but interiorly, he wandered away from his father. He did his duty, worked hard every day, and fulfilled all his obligations but became increasingly unhappy and unfree.[37]

The elder brother appears more virtuous but stews in his resentment and also stands in need of his father's merciful love. He's one of those people who, in the words of Benedict XVI:

> . . . need to convert from the Law-God to the greater God of love. This will not mean giving up their obedience, but rather that this obedience will flow from deeper

---

37. Nouwen, p. 69.

wellsprings and will therefore be bigger, more open, and purer, but above all more humble.[38]

The elder son's conversion, though, is more complicated. "Returning home from a lustful escapade seems so much easier than returning home from a cold anger that has rooted itself in the deepest corners of my being."[39] The misconduct of the elder is more difficult to acknowledge, since his egotism is concealed beneath his desire to be virtuous.

The father also has compassion for the elder son. Rather than reproach him, he goes out to meet him and ease his conversion. He recalls his incomparable dignity as son: "Son, you are always with me, and all that is mine is yours," he assures him (Lk 15:31). The parable doesn't indicate whether the elder brother converts in the end, but we can venture a hypothesis. If his perfectionism is very deep-rooted, he'll find it difficult. So it is with those who have been very demanding with themselves, but not for love of God. Pride interferes with their ability to be tolerant with themselves. They only enjoy a modicum of inner peace when they are satisfied that they've done everything just right. They cannot discern the predilection God has for people who acknowledge their neediness. Falling into the same trap as the elder brother, after years of exemplary behavior, they cannot bear either others' flaws or their own lack of rectitude of intention being exposed.

Still, this very despair can create an opening for the beginnings of a turnaround. This is the second hypothesis about the elder brother's fate. For this to ensue, he must be convinced that his paradigms have failed, abdicate his self-sufficiency,

---

38. Benedict XVI, *Jesus of Nazareth* (New York: Doubleday, 2007), pp. 210–211.
39. Nouwen, p. 75.

and then discover, by grace, that the only thing worthwhile is giving and receiving genuine love. This trusting surrender frees the soul from its slavery to pride.

PURITY OF INTENTION IN THE CHRISTIAN LIFE

The bottom line is that the elder son does not have a pure intention. His pride has contaminated the scrupulous performance of his moral duties. Instead of seeking the good of others, out of love, he focuses egotistically on his own excellence. In the Christian life we too can fall into this same perfectionistic moralism. In one of her novels, Sigrid Undset portrays an exemplary religious who one day realizes that "pride, and not meekness or thankfulness for Jesus' redeeming death, had held her up . . . self-righteousness had she spread thick upon her dry bread, while the other sisters were drinking their beer and eating their bread-slices with butter."[40] It's tricky to detect these egocentric intentions. There are certain symptoms—such as a feeling of oppression when it comes time to carry out one's resolutions—but they're perceptible only with a keen and courageous examination of conscience. St. Josemaría writes:

> The motives that inspire you, even in the holiest actions, do not seem clear, and deep down inside you hear a voice which makes you see human reasons, in such a subtle way that your soul is invaded by the disturbing thought that you don't act as you should. . . . React at once each

40. Sigrid Undset, *The Bridal Wreath: Kristin Lavransdatter* (New York: Random House/ First Vintage Books Edition, 1987).

time and say, "Lord, for myself I want nothing. All for your glory and for Love."[41]

Pride sometimes causes people to turn the Christian life itself into a means of satisfying selfish ambition. Even those who have surrendered their lives to God and then pursued positions of responsibility may overburden people beneath them with a merciless and cruel spirit. They longed for a grand ideal; perhaps that's why it's so hard for them to realize that what they're seeking is not so much God's glory as their own self-affirmation. "I lived for man on the pretext of living for God," acknowledges a priest in a Tolstoy novella.[42] A deformed intention can subtly corrupt even the noblest desires. We can observe this in another story:

> He's a religious who will never skip an hour of prayer, or break a precept, or dispute an order—a perfect career religious. . . . However, he's a man without a heart. In its place is the law, and, concealed behind that, ambition: terrible, devouring ambition.[43]

Pride creates an obstacle to understanding the nature of sanctity. It is not a *general perfection*, but a *perfection of love*, an effective concern for pleasing the Lord. It leads as much to humbly allowing oneself to be loved with all one's shortcomings as to heroically striving for growth in virtue. Holiness is not *achieved*; it's *received*. It's an abundance God grants to those who acknowledge their hollowness and allow God to fill them. "Clearly the heart of holiness is the question of

41. Escrivá, *The Way* (New York: Scepter, 1992), no. 788.
42. Tolstoy, *Father Sergius and Other Stories* (New York: Dodd, Mead and Company, 1912), p. 88.
43. S. Martín, *El suicidio de San Francisco* (Barcelona: Planeta, 1998), pp. 177–178.

trust: what a man is disposed to let God do in him. It's not so much the 'I do' as the 'Be it done unto me.' "[44] This "be it done" is not passivity but active cooperation with the Holy Spirit, whose grace sanctifies us through inner transformation. The Virgin Mary is the best example of all. Her "Let it be to me according to your word" (Lk 1:38) is the most sublime expression of loving surrender to God's desires. This is why the Lord was—and is—able to work wonders in and through her (see Lk 1:49).

St. Josemaría distinguishes between good and bad "divinization,"[45] depending on whether the spiritual edifice rests on a foundation of humility or pride. If it's pride, the desire for improvement entails an unwholesome anxiety for self-affirmation, in which pleasing God is all but forgotten. At its root, it conceals an unfulfilled self, impossible to satisfy. Its dictatorship precludes all inner peace, since pride demands great sacrifices and is never content. It's like an inner voice that scolds us for the tiniest faults, like a wet blanket who won't stop pestering us. Such an outlook can lead to moral legalism, making us forget that "a Christian is not a neurotic collector of good behaviour reports."[46] Thus, the better conceals the worse.

Humble self-esteem rules out boastfulness as well as comparisons with others. Free of these, we're no longer preoccupied by our own merits, and nothing prevents our rejoicing at others' success. But whoever succumbs to the tyranny of pride feels the need to be certain of being better than others—like the Pharisee in the parable who comes to the temple to pray

---

44. Urbano, *El hombre de villa tevere*, p. 168.
45. See Escrivá, *Friends of God*, no. 94.
46. Escrivá, *Christ Is Passing By*, no. 75.

beside the publican. The Pharisee feels superior and, gloating over his virtues, prays as follows: "God, I thank thee that I am not like other men: extortioners, unjust, adulterers, or even like this tax collector. I fast twice a week, I give tithes of all that I get" (Lk 18: 11–12).

However, pride's ability to corrupt even the noblest desires is no excuse for ceasing to desire perfection. It's better to aspire to holiness incorrectly than to sit by in idle passivity. One needs to move beyond this imperfect stage of love, purifying it, with the peace of feeling sheltered by the loving gaze of God. St. Thérèse of Lisieux said that the Lord told her not to keep track of her virtuous actions but simply to turn any daily circumstance, however little, into an occasion of loving him.

> At this moment, your Thérèse does not find herself on the heights, but Jesus is teaching her. . . . He is teaching her to play at love's bank, or rather, he plays for her, not telling her just how he goes about it, for that is his business, not Thérèse's; her part is to abandon herself, to give herself over, keeping nothing for herself, not even the joy of knowing how his bank is paying.[47]

RECIPROCITY: IN TUNE WITH THE BELOVED

The lack of purity of intention is not due solely to pride. It also reveals a lack of harmony with the beloved. In the parable of the prodigal son, the elder brother is indeed deficient in humility but, on top of that, he has failed to understand the love that drives his father's continual concern for the

---

47. Hans Urs Von Balthasar, *Two Sisters in the Spirit: Thérèse of Lisieux & Elizabeth of the Trinity* (San Francisco: Ignatius, 1992), p. 253.

well-being of both his sons—while each of them goes his own way, oblivious to the sorrow or joy he might be causing. The parable reveals not only the homeward path the prodigal son ought to take, but also the enormous pain his waywardness causes his father—this "self-inflicted wound."[48] Throughout the son's absence, "his father lives in continual worry: he awaits him, hoping for his return, scanning the horizon. He respects his son's freedom; still, he suffers."[49] This is the positive side of the bitterness of our offenses against God, the proof that he loves us. "He is a God who rejoices at our affection and is pained by our coldness."[50]

Neither brother understands how to put himself in his father's shoes. The prodigal is surprised at the magnanimity with which he is received. In all his contrivances to return, he had planned on working as just one more hired hand, so as to expiate his guilt. Had he known that his father spent his days scanning the horizon for him, he would have returned far sooner. The elder brother's attitude likewise leaves much to be desired. He is oblivious to how his cold and "irreproachable" conduct also brings suffering upon his father. Both sons would do well to think less about their own personal problems and more about the pain they are inflicting on their father by distancing themselves from him. Whether physically remote or withdrawn into pride, they would then hasten back home to him. Péguy puts these words into God's mouth: "You make me wait so long. You make me wait too long for penitence after your fall and for contrition after your sin."[51]

---

48. Urbano, *La madre*, p. 38.
49. John Paul II, Message for 14th World Youth Day, 1999, no. 4.
50. Echevarría, *Itinerarios de vida cristiana*, p. 89.
51. In Manglano, *Orar con poetas* (Bilbao: Desclée de Brouwer, 1999), p. 140.

We are often prone to slip out of harmony with the Lord. "Ordinarily," observes Javier Echevarría, "we regard God as the source and content of our peace—which is true, but not the whole truth. We don't tend to think, for example, that we too *can* console God and offer him a resting place. But this is how the saints have acted."[52] Gustave Thibon goes further. During an interview towards the end of his life, he declared: "For too long, men have prayed to a Caesar-God; it is high time for them to hear the prayer of a slave-God. . . . After a religion of God's mercy upon men, will we see a religion that sinks its roots into man's mercy upon God?"[53]

Love demands reciprocity: We can love somebody who doesn't love us in return, but in that case it is impossible to establish a love *relationship*. The same is true of friendship: we cannot be friends with someone who doesn't want to be friends with us. To establish a *reciprocal relationship of love with God* is of ultimate importance to the Christian life. As Bl. John Paul II affirmed on the cusp of the new millennium, "This reciprocity is the very substance and soul of the Christian life."[54]

Those who haven't learned to be in touch with God's loving expectations are destined to live a superficial Christian life. Like the two sons in the parable, they would treat the Lord better if they were aware of his loving vulnerability. Those who are ignorant of this mysterious reality approach the Lord only when they have some petition, oblivious to how much they can offer him. Others don't pray at all: they don't practice their faith and end up reducing it to a mere

---

52. Echevarría, *Eucaristía y vida cristiana* (Madrid: Rialp, 2005), 2nd ed., p. 203.
53. Thibon, in *L'Agora*, 5, 1998.
54. John Paul II, *Novo millenio ineunte*, no. 32.

matter of ethics. They manage a vague adherence to certain moral values, without realizing that the first commandment is "You shall love the Lord your God with all your heart, and with all your soul, and with all your mind, and with all your strength" (Mk 12:30; see Mt 22:37 and Lk 10:27). And this is not merely a moral imperative. The chief motivation behind our efforts ought to be inspired by the loving desire to please our Father-God, to avoid making him suffer by the pain we cause ourselves when we sin. Commenting on the conversion of St. Paul, André Frossard rightly affirms:

> Christianity is not a conception of the world, nor even a rule of life: it is a love story that begins anew with each soul. For the greatest of the apostles, fascinated to the end by a face glimpsed on the road to Damascus, the truth is not an idea to be served, but a person to be loved.[55]

Being in touch with this divine expectancy is also a great aid to consistent Christians—those who, wishing to love the Lord with all their heart, strive to advance in their prayer life. All the baptized are called to holiness: to love God and others *as much and as well as possible.* But if we're oblivious to the pain and joy we procure for the Lord, we can fall into two possible extremes: either the lukewarmness of not wanting to complicate our life, or else a voluntaristic surrender. Imagine a person who strives to fulfill faithfully all his religious obligations and all the duties of his state of life. Every Sunday he punctually arrives at Mass; he confesses regularly; he doesn't harm anyone—in fact, he tries to behave as well as possible with others; he has absorbing work but doesn't

---

55. Frossard, *Los grandes pastores* (Madrid: Rialp, 1993), p. 115.

neglect his family. . . . If we tell him that all this is not
enough and encourage him to intensify his dealings with the
Lord, or find time to attend means of Christian formation or
retreats . . . he may say to us (if he's not inclined to be insecure or a perfectionist) that he sees no reason to complicate
his life so much. But he might see things differently if, besides
explaining to him that closeness to the Lord will enrich all
his earthly love and make it happier, we help him to see the
urgency of God's ardent love for *him*. As St. John Chrysostom
observes, "Nothing moves one to love so much as the thought
on the beloved's part that the lover desires greatly to have his
love requited."[56] The needs of others incite our generosity. If
we see someone we love weeping, we hasten to console him,
just as a mother comes to ease her child's suffering, sparing
no effort. One father who was a heavy sleeper told me of the
paradoxical sacrifice it would have been for him *not* to go to
his little children if he heard them crying. On the other hand,
how hard it is to love those who don't allow themselves to be
loved! Nothing is so discouraging as the impossibility of offering the beloved anything. "Who knows how completely love
can repress all our strength until suddenly we lose the chance
to help the one we love most?"[57]

We do well to meditate on the repercussions of our moral
acts on God's own suffering and rejoicing. The pain of the
father in the parable (an image of the divine) is pure, his joy
intense. Faced with offenses, he doesn't compile a list of griev-
ances. He's concerned only for his sons' happiness. He suffers when they stray and rejoices when they return. Upon the
arrival of the younger, he instructs the elder: "It was fitting to

56. John Chrysostom, Homily 14, 1.
57. J. Dobraczynski, *Cartas a Nicodemo* (Barcelona: Herder, 1990), p. 17.

make merry and be glad, for this your brother was dead, and is alive; he was lost, and is found" (Lk 15:32). His joy is commensurate with his love, and God always loves infinitely. We are everything to him; he loves us as he loves himself.

Some object that God cannot suffer; one of his essential attributes is his impassibility. It is, therefore, vital to develop a *theology of the suffering of God.* Clearly, the Divine Being is not subject to passions, since, as St. Irenaeus puts it, "He is rich, perfect, and without any indigence."[58] He has no needs. But, having created us out of love, the only thing he "lacks" (so to speak) is our love. As the *Catechism* affirms, "God thirsts that we may thirst for him."[59] He desires our happiness—something that is only possible if we respond to his love. Thus, there arises a mysterious "indigence" which implies no imperfection. In a single act of creation and love, God chooses to bestow being on man because he loves him.

The divine perfection is not diminished by this mysterious, loving indigence. The one doesn't cancel out the other. Love leads one to identify oneself with the joys and sorrows of the beloved. In God, this identification is infinite. Those who love expose themselves to the experiences of joy and sorrow. Love, depending on whether it is requited, always entails gratitude or disappointment. God, too, in creating us out of love, "has made himself accessible and, therefore, vulnerable as well."[60] The passion of Christ is the maximum revelation of God the Father's enormous suffering at the harm we inflict on ourselves when we sin. As Bl. John Paul II notes:

---

58. Irenaeus, *Adversus Haereses*, Book IV, 13, 4:SC 100, p. 534.
59. *Catechism of the Catholic Church*, 2560.
60. Benedict XVI, *Jesus of Nazareth*, pp. 143–144.

[O]ften, the Sacred Book speaks to us of a Father who feels compassion for man, as though sharing his pain. In a word, this inscrutable and indescribable fatherly "pain" will bring about above all the wonderful economy of redemptive love in Jesus Christ . . . in whose humanity the "suffering" of God is concretized.[61]

Divine *impassibility*, in other words, doesn't mean *indifference*. As Pope Benedict XVI recalls:

The Christian faith . . . has shown us that God—Truth and Love in person—desired to suffer for us and with us. Bernard of Clairvaux coined the marvelous expression: *Impassibilis est Deus, sed non incompassibilis*[62]—God cannot suffer, but he can *suffer with*.[63]

We find ourselves, then, before a great mystery. God is at once impassible and compassionate, transcendent and "entangled" in the world, absolute (not contingent on anyone) and freely united to us all with bonds of love. Our intellect cannot comprehend how both realities can coexist in God. The divine is unimaginable, but no less real for that. What is certain is that all our amazement is dwarfed by the ineffable reality.

Like the Virgin Mary, intoning the Magnificat, we cannot get over our amazement if we realize that we, who are worth so little, matter to God so much (see Lk 1:46–55).

---

61. John Paul II, *Dominum et vivificantem*, no. 39.

62. *Sermones in Cant., Sermo* 26, 5: *PL* 183, 906.

63. Benedict XVI, *Spes salvi*, no. 39. See also *Jesus of Nazareth*, [p. 116 in Spanish edition] and *Deus caritas est*, nos. 9–10.

5.

Various Manifestations of the Love of God

Since God loves us so deeply and unconditionally, why are we still so often full of worry and unrest? Why are we not all radically transformed? It may be because our knowledge of God is purely theoretical. We wouldn't be indifferent if someone told us they'd transferred a hundred million euros into a Swiss bank account to be paid out in two million fifty-euro bills. It's easy to love God passionately when we grasp the depth of his love. As Dietrich von Hildebrand writes:

> That Christ loves us is the great secret, the most intimate secret of every soul. It is the most inconceivable reality; it is a reality that would change the life of anyone who fully took it in. But in order to take it in fully, one needs more than a mere theoretical knowledge, but rather a lived experience of that love like the experience one has of the love of a beloved person.[1]

---

1. Von Hildebrand, *The Heart*, p. 16.

KNOWING, SENSING, AND FEELING

In the words of Benedict XVI, each of us needs the "experience of being loved by Jesus Christ in a totally personal way."[2] "Although it is not a question of sentiment," says St. Josemaría, "little by little the love of God makes itself felt like a rustle in the soul."[3] To be touched by something is much deeper than feeling or knowing. A Japanese saying illustrates the difference well: "When a child dies, acquaintances suffer with the head, friends with the heart, the mother, in all the depth of her core." As Benedict XVI teaches, we must penetrate more and more into the heart of Christ:

> Thus, we will be able to understand better what it means *to know* God's love in Jesus Christ, *to experience* him, keeping our gaze fixed on him to the point that we *live* entirely on the experience of his love, so that we can subsequently *witness* to it to others.[4]

This profound awareness of God's love is forged, little by little, throughout life. It's the mysterious effect of the action of grace together with our response. This collaboration is made concrete especially when we're striving to improve our interior dispositions, since, as Benedict XVI notes, "True knowledge of God's love is only possible in the context of an attitude of humble prayer and generous availability."[5] Our response to grace also translates into a daily effort to seek, converse with, and love the Lord. With time, his companionship becomes

---

2. Benedict XVI, Homily, June 28, 2008 (Inauguration of the Pauline Year).

3. Escrivá, *Christ Is Passing By*, no. 8.

4. Benedict XVI, Letter, May 15, 2006, in commemoration of the 50th anniversary of the encyclical *Haurietis aquas*.

5. Benedict XVI, Letter, May 15, 2006.

a necessity. If we don't neglect our times of prayer, the Lord gradually steals our heart and, as St. Josemaría puts it:

> This gives way to intimacy with God, looking at God without needing rest or feeling tired. We begin to live as captives, as prisoners. And while we carry out as perfectly as we can (with all our mistakes and limitations) the tasks allotted to us by our situation and duties, our soul longs to escape. It is drawn towards God like iron drawn by a magnet. One begins to love Jesus, in a more effective way, with the sweet and gentle surprise of his encounter.[6]

To facilitate this action of grace, let us now examine the manifestations of God's love that confer the greatest dignity: divine filiation, the Incarnation, and the Redemption. One and the same love leads God to create us, to make us his children, and, after our rejection, to become incarnate in order to redeem us.

DIVINE FILIATION

The way for a Christian to become aware of his dignity *par excellence* comes by way of awareness of his or her divine filiation in Christ. If God is the great King of the Universe, then we, his children, are princes and princesses. And this is no mere honorific title—it's a joyful reality. Already, in the Old Testament, God begins to reveal his love for each and every person. He tells us, through the prophet Isaiah, "Fear not, for I have redeemed you; I have called you by name, you are mine. . . . Because you are precious in my eyes, and honored, and I love you" (Is 43:1, 4). What was latent in the

---

6. Escrivá, *Friends of God*, no. 296.

Old Covenant is made patent with Christ. St. John marvels when he reflects on our incomparable dignity; he exclaims, "See what love the Father has given us, that we should be called children of God; and so we are" (1 Jn 3:1). "We are not orphans; love is possible. Because—as you know—we are not capable of loving if we are not loved."[7]

We can never meditate enough on this blessed truth. St. Leo the Great captured it: "Christian, remember your dignity, and now that you share in God's own nature (see 2 Pt 1:4), do not return by sin to your former base condition . . . for your liberty was bought by the blood of Christ."[8] All amazement falls short. It is worth considering assiduously, as St. Josemaría exclaimed about divine filiation: "What a strange capacity man has to forget even the most wonderful things, to become used to mystery!"[9]

The divinization that Christ has promised us opens up marvelous new perspectives. "The only-begotten Son of God," taught Thomas Aquinas, "wanting to make us sharers in his divinity, assumed our nature, so that he, made man, might make men gods."[10] He wants to divinize us! If we're not more astonished by this marvel, perhaps it's because we don't think it's meant literally. Speaking of these promises, St. Peter writes that the Word was incarnate to make us "partakers of the divine nature" (2 Pt 1:4). St. Athanasius confirms it: "God became man so that man might become God."[11] We don't understand

---

7. John Paul II, Message for the 14th World Youth Day (1999), no. 3.

8. Leo the Great, Homily 1 on Christmas (In the Divine Office, 2nd reading of December 25).

9. Escrivá, *Christ Is Passing By*, no. 65.

10. Aquinas, *Opus. 57 in Festo Corporis Christi*, lect. 1.

11. Athanasius of Alexandria, *In incarnatione*, 54, 3.

how it's possible to divinize a human being, but we know that if God became truly man without ceasing to be God, he can accomplish it "the other way around." The structure of the human person might be compared to a building on whose roof one can continue building as far as heaven—as far as God.

As simple human beings, our worth is small, but God has destined us to be freely exalted through a gift that can divinize us. If we use our freedom well and accept the divine offer, we receive the greatest dignity imaginable: that of being children of God. As Javier Echevarría notes, "Divine filiation, God's call to be his sons and daughters in Jesus Christ, is a treasure not to be compared, in its richness, with even the most precious earthly good."[12] Anyone who grasps such dignity will experience that wholesome pride of a child of God that made St. John of the Cross exclaim, with justified daring, "Mine are the heavens and mine is the earth. . . . What do you ask, then, and seek, my soul? Yours is all of this, and all is for you."[13]

Like Little Children

Divine filiation is the *foundation* of the Christian life. If we know we're the children of such a benevolent Father, we will treat him with trusting familiarity and abandon ourselves confidently to him. Each and every one of our actions is thus lit up with meaning. We may understand better if we observe a little child with his father: with what implicit trust he attracts his attention, draws a smile from him, rejoices to be with him, or coaxes a caress. This is how we too can imagine the ineffable glance of our most loving Father. If we do this often,

---

12. Echevarría, *Itinerarios*, p. 11.
13. St. John of the Cross, *Prayer of a Soul Taken with Love*.

living in God's presence becomes a necessity to our soul. As St. Josemaría tells us:

> The Lord, by loving us as his children, has taken us into his house, in the middle of the world, to be members of his family, so that what is his is ours, and what is ours is his, and to develop that familiarity and confidence which prompts us to ask him, like children, for the moon![14]

"As a father pities his children, so the Lord pities those who fear him," says the psalmist (Ps 103:13). The analogy of human fatherhood helps us deepen our understanding of the divine goodness. Any anecdote along these lines serves to illustrate. A child's first drawing, for instance, is much more than a scribble in the eyes of a father, who will examine it with much attentive curiosity and even more affection. In the same way, nothing we do is insignificant in God's eyes. We won't focus so much on the value of our "drawing" as on the merciful love with which he looks upon it. St. Bernard is completely right to say, "My merit therefore is the mercy of the Lord. Surely I am not devoid of merit as long as he is not of mercy. And if the Lord abounds in mercy, I too must abound in merits."[15] The value of our little gifts is multiplied by the greatness of God's love for us. It's like the help that a little child insists on giving to his father to carry the groceries into the house. It's clear that the child doesn't have the strength to carry much, but his father gives him a bag with a few light objects to make him believe his collaboration is crucial. The child feels important, and his father is moved at his generosity.

---

14. *Christ Is Passing By*, no. 64.
15. Bernard de Clairvaux, *In Cantica Canticorum*, Sermon 61, 5.

Without Fear

Knowing we're children of such a good Father helps correct our notion of the fear of God and purify the pride that blunts our desire to progress in the Christian life. Conceit causes us to distort God's intentions for his creatures, "placing in doubt the truth about God who is Love and leaving man only with the sense of the master-slave relationship."[16] Given this false image of God, some rebel against him. Others do not abandon him, but they submit to him with a slave's mentality. They limit themselves to fulfilling their religious duties out of fear of punishment. They think they will be disgraced before a God whom they see above all as a dominator. This servile fear is born, ultimately, of having conceived of God's love as something small and stingy.

Four thousand years ago, people had wandered far from the truth. In revealing himself, God, like a good teacher, proceeded by stages. The Old Testament may be compared to elementary school, the New Testament to high school. In the Old Testament, without much nuance, the most basic truths are introduced: the greatness of God the Creator and the consequent *reverential fear*, or attitude of profound respect and praise, that he deserves. In the New Testament, Jesus Christ, revealing to us the depths of God's love, teaches us a new type of *filial fear*, proper to one who knows he is a child of God and only fears wounding his father's heart. The new does not abrogate the old—it transcends it (see Mt 5:17). Similarly, filial fear doesn't exclude reverential fear; thus, in Christian catechesis, before speaking of divine filiation, one needs to foster a profound respect for God, who has created us and

---

16. John Paul II, *Threshold*, p. 228.

will judge us. It's not a question of inculcating *servile fear*, but rather an attitude of respect for the sacred and a horror of blasphemy. Knowing that God is going to judge me could inspire excessive fear, but if I am realistic, I will realize that the one I should fear is not God, but myself, since I can make evil use of my freedom and deprive myself of the eternal gift he wants to give me.

A deep internalization of the reality of divine filiation is the best remedy for servile fear. St. Josemaría used to say that he knew no fear of God other than the kind a son suffers when he has displeased his father. If we're aware of the constant and attentive closeness of so good a God, "there's no room anymore for a cold and fearful attitude, somewhere between pharisaical and puritanical, which reduces religion to a mere effort to stay "on the good side" of a God of severity. Nor is there room for superficiality or routine in our dealings with God."[17]

Beneath scrupulous and perfectionistic religious attitudes, one always finds an explosive mix of good will, self-righteousness, and servile fear. This fear excludes love: "He who fears is not perfected in love," pronounces St. John (1 Jn 4:18). "For us, the fear of God consists wholly in love."[18]

The lack of harmony with the loving intentions of God the Father sometimes brings with it a deep uneasiness. This can be observed in people who are temperamentally insecure and unconsciously "shrink" the love of God. What ought to be their liberation becomes their chains. Their relationship with God has turned into one more burden. If they were in touch with his love, they would be tremendously joyful.

---

17. Echevarría, *Itinerarios*, p. 16.
18. St. Hilary, "Fear of the Lord" (Ps. 127: 1–3).

Instead, they reduce the Christian life to "a set of oppressive rules which leave the soul in a state of exasperation and tension."[19] Ultimately, it is the lack of humble self-esteem that makes a relationship with God deteriorate and leads to all kinds of headaches. Some are so overwhelmed by their efforts to improve themselves that they would rather succumb to idleness than keep up the struggle. Others keep striving, but in a perfectionist way; their efforts are motivated mostly by an excessive desire to get "on the right side" of God.

Gratuitous and Unconditional

Those who become overwhelmed by the demands of the Christian life ought to meditate assiduously on the qualities of God's love. Above all, it is *gratuitous*. It always precedes our own. He doesn't love us because we deserve it, but because he is good. He's not expecting us to measure up. He's waiting, rather, for us to abdicate our self-sufficiency and accept his love. If a professor gave final grades at the outset, there would be no sense in doing extra-credit work. God doesn't ask us to love him as a condition of his loving us more, but because he knows that we'll be happy if we unite ourselves lovingly to him. He loves us "more than all the mothers in the world can love their children."[20] And he does so *unconditionally*, as one loves an only child. You might say that God only knows how to have only children. He loves us, at each moment, just as we are. Even if we became a hundred times better or a hundred times worse than we are now, he wouldn't love us any more or any less, since already, right now, he loves us with all his immense capacity to love. Even if we

19. Escrivá, *Friends of God*, no. 137.
20. Escrivá, *The Way*, no. 267.

were to work at offending him, we'd never succeed in making him stop loving us. What we can prevent, since he respects our liberty, is his love reaching us (i.e., it does no good for him to love us if we don't let ourselves be loved).

God's love is key to growing in *rectitude of intention*. Knowing we are loved so much confers on us an extraordinary dignity, which slakes our thirst for appreciation. Self-forgetfulness is easy when we remember that subjectively we're everything to the One who objectively is all in all. Knowing that we're the objects of divine pleasure, we're able to purify our desires for self-improvement. We're able to act purely for him, not to satisfy our own pride. God's love frees us from our own vanity; it makes us capable of doing all things for love of him and others. We'll act first of all for him, to give him pleasure—since, although by his nature he lacks nothing, having created us out of love, we could say that our love is the only thing "wanting" in him. This mutual love will reach its height in heaven with an eternal union of love.

In the end, God's love seeks to be *requited*. It seems audacious to imagine an equal relationship with God, even if it is his love that elevates us to his own level. Ineffably but truly, his love brings him to identify himself with everything in us, everything that concerns us. If we conduct ourselves viciously, it pains him unspeakably, and if we love him and allow him to love us, we procure an infinite joy for him. This pain and joy are unimaginable but, as we shall see next, the Incarnation facilitates it all.

MUTUAL FRIENDSHIP WITH CHRIST

The path to God culminates with a deep sense of our divine filiation, but it is fitting that it happens by way of an intimate friendship with Jesus Christ. In this way, it is much easier to establish a *mutual relation of love* and really "put ourselves in his shoes." God "feels" infinitely more than we do, even if this reality is an unfathomable mystery. We have no idea what the pain and joy of an infinite being are like, but the sentiments of Jesus are perfectly imaginable. Thus, he refers to himself as "the way" (Jn 14:6) to the Father.

"It makes me very happy to realize that Christ wanted to be fully a man, with flesh like our own. I am moved when I contemplate how wonderful it is for God to love with a man's heart."[21] No wonder we are astonished at a God who, being so great, makes himself so small. We are startled to reflect on the omnipotent God who is born in Bethlehem as a helpless, needy infant. The fact that God deigns to share our humble nature *dignifies* us; it makes clear how much we matter to him and "how great each man has become through this mystery."[22] But before considering why we should be so grateful for the Incarnation, it is worth making a brief theological digression into God's revelations about it.

True God and True Man

Twenty centuries ago, the Word, consubstantial with the Father, took on an integral human nature, making himself a man like us "yet without sin" (Heb 4:15). Christ is thus "true God and true man."[23] His two natures are infinitely distinct but subsist in one and the same person (the Second Person of the Blessed Trinity). Jesus Christ is perfect God and perfect man. He is not "less" God for having become man, nor "less"

---

21. Escrivá, *Christ Is Passing By*, no. 198.
22. John Paul II, Angelus at Czestochowa, June 5, 1979.
23. See *CCC*, 456–483.

man for being God. Since there are two natures in him, there are also two intellects and two wills.

As the liturgy affirms, Christ's two natures are joined "without mixture or division."[24] This means that he is neither some sort of human-divine hybrid nor two persons united like Siamese twins. The Magisterium teaches that the two natures are united "without confusion, change, division, or separation."[25] "Without confusion" means that the Word has assumed human nature without absorbing it;[26] that is, that the human nature is in no way negated by the divine. It preserves, for example, all the imperatives proper to a perfect human heart. If God were an ocean and man a drop of water, the Incarnation would mean that the *ocean*, without ceasing to be an ocean, had made itself at the same time a *water drop*, without dissolving into it. It might work better to speak of a *drop of oil* in an ocean of water.[27]

Since Christ's two natures are neither mixed nor confused, it's possible to treat him as a man without forgetting that he's also God. And it's fitting for us to do just that since, as a man, he shares our feelings—which makes it much easier to be "in sync" with him. Without lacking in due respect, we can treat him as our best friend, with great freedom and trust, as an equal. This allows us, for instance, as we draw near to

---

24. Liturgy of the Hours, Lauds, January 1, Antiphon, "Ad Benedictus."

25. Council of Chalcedon, Denzinger, no. 302.

26. See Vatican II, *Gaudium et spes*, no. 22.

27. In fact, there are two possible mistakes to be avoided: treating Jesus Christ as if he were not truly man, or as if he were not truly God. The first would amount, in practice, to falling into the ancient heresy of monophysitism; the second, into the even more ancient heresy of Arianism. Whoever denies Christ's human nature tends to treat him with great respect but no familiarity. Those who don't believe in his divinity tend to speak of "Jesus of Nazareth" in the same detached tones they would use for Socrates or any other historical figure.

a tabernacle, reflecting on his divinity and real presence, to kneel down with great respect—and at the same time, we can speak to him with simplicity and familiarity, as we would with a good friend. Our dealings with Mary, if we've learned to love her as her children, may initially seem easier: Although she is the most holy Mother of God, she's a creature like ourselves. Besides, she's our mother, and it's not hard to confide in a good mother. We experience the same thing if we know how to draw near to Christ's sacred humanity. Thus St. Josemaría's advice: "Don't be afraid to call our Lord by his name— Jesus—and to tell him that you love him."[28]

This ease in relating to and loving the Lord is a clear reason for gratitude. St. Josemaría exclaimed, "I give you thanks, my Jesus, for your decision to become perfect Man, with a Heart which loved and is most loveable, which loved unto death and suffered, which was filled with joy and sorrow."[29] God didn't become incarnate only to fulfill revelation and bring about the Redemption, but also to draw closer and be more accessible to us. François Mauriac admits wholeheartedly:

> If I had not come to know Christ, God would be a meaningless word for me. Without some very particular grace, infinite Being would be unimaginable to me. The God of the philosophers and the intellectuals would have no role to play in my moral life.[30]

God's love is indescribable, but Christ reveals it to us with words we can understand. What is most noble can penetrate

---

28. Escrivá, *The Way*, no. 303.

29. Escrivá, *Furrow*, no. 813.

30. F. Mauriac, *Vida De Jesus: Novela* (Barcelona: Plaza & Janes Editores, 1976); see J. Herranz, *En las afueras de Jericó* (Madrid: Rialp, 2007), p. 408.

us only through tangible realities. With the Incarnation, notes St. Leo the Great, "He who was invisible by his nature becomes visible in our own; he who was inaccessible to our mind wished to make himself accessible; he who existed before time began to exist in time."[31] It is now possible to relate to the divine by means of the human. The Christ-Man is like a small copy of the immense tenderness of God the Father. We were created in his image and likeness, but in the most holy humanity of Christ the resemblance is closer. The moon only shines with reflected light from the sun but, since it's less brilliant, we can see it better.

In Harmony with Christ's Sentiments

It's easy to love Christ if, aware of "the full significance of Christ's Incarnation,"[32] we discern the affections that inflame his heart.[33] "In Christ," recalls Bl. John Paul II, "God has truly assumed . . . a human heart, capable of all the stirrings of affection."[34] It is worth meditating upon the Gospel to get an idea of "the holy affectivity of Christ's most Sacred Humanity."[35] His extraordinary affective capacity is manifested in an abundance of little touches: He embraces children

31. Leo the Great, Letter 28 to Flavian, 4.

32. Escrivá, *Friends of God*, no. 74.

33. Here there is a parallel between the order of grace and the order of experience. Identification with Christ is both the starting point and the goal. Baptism, by making us children of God, constitutes each of us as "another Christ" (see Gal 2:19–20). As his brothers and sisters, we are called to share in his heart's affections. The identification with Christ that grace confers ought to be accompanied, in practice, by an effort to unite ourselves lovingly to his most sacred humanity.

34. John Paul II, *Rosarium virginis Mariae*, no. 26.

35. Von Hildebrand, *The Heart*, p. 22.

(see Mk 9:36), loves his friends (see Jn 11:15), and is deeply moved when Lazarus dies (see Jn 11:33–35, 38); he looks with affection on the rich young man (see Mk 10:21), and he is concerned that his disciples rest in a family atmosphere (see Mk 6:31). Especially notable is his compassion for those who suffer (see Mt 9:2; Mt 9:36; Mk 6:34).

We recall, as an illustration, how he took charge of the widow of Nain, who was burying her only son. "And when the Lord saw her," recounts St. Luke, "he had compassion on her and said to her 'Do not weep'" (Lk 7:13). Moved by one of these "reasons of the heart that reason knows not of,"[36] Jesus makes an exception: He raises the son to life without asking the mother for a sign of faith. The miracle, comments St. Josemaría, was a "sign of the power of Christ who is God. But first came his compassion, an evident sign of the tenderness of the heart of Christ the man."[37]

Reflection also helps us gain a sense of *how*—and *how much*—Jesus feels. There is, indeed, a difference in *intensity* and in *quality* between the sentiments of the resurrected Christ and our own. Our actions affect him with a power proportional to his love. The more perfect a human being, the greater his or her affective capacity, though no human sentiment is infinite. Thus, Jesus' affection will be multiple times more powerful than that of the most saintly human being who ever existed. Putting a number to it may make it more accessible: if the heart of Jesus were a hundred times greater than our own, what happens to us will affect him, for better or for worse, a hundredfold. There's also a qualitative difference between Christ's feelings and our own. We've already

---

36. See Blaise Pascal, *Pensées* (London: Penguin Classics, 1995).
37. Escrivá, *Christ Is Passing By*, no. 166.

seen that our own joys and sorrows are associated with our pride as much as with our heart. In him, by contrast, there's no egotism at all. His joys are free of vanity; his pain has nothing to do with wounded pride. He rejoices and suffers solely because he loves us. No feeling of joy or sorrow is as beautiful as those of the heart of Jesus.

If we are in sync with his heart, we'll feel the need to shower him with joys, by our generous surrender as well as our humble contrition. "Abide in me, and I in you," Jesus says to us (Jn 15:4). He never ceases to love us. Thus, we feel compelled to offer him joys and to console him for the pain our sins cause him—our own as well as others'. If we grasp the weight of this sorrow, we will feel great sorrow ourselves. Commenting on the Passion, José Pedro Manglano cries, "How I love to see you like this! In need of consolation! . . . I believe there is nothing greater than a God who inspires pity . . . if the pity comes from love."[38] This pain is an effective spur to our generosity. What a beautiful thing it is to dry the tears of someone weeping! Coaxing a smile from an unhappy face is like causing a brilliant sun to shine out suddenly in the midst of a cloudy sky.

Lope de Vega summarizes Christ's burning expectation of love in one of his most famous sonnets:

What have I to offer, that you should seek my friendship?
What interest pursues you, my Jesus,
That at my dew-drenched door
You pass the black winter nights?

---

38. Manglano, *Se puede aprender a sufrir?* (Desclée de Brouwer: Bilbao, 1999), pp. 52, 56.

Oh, how cold my heart was,

For I would not open to you! What strange caprice

If by my ingratitude the frosty ice

Dried the wounded soles of your pure feet

How often did the angel say to me:

Soul, hasten to the window:

You'll see with what persistent love he calls you

And how often, sovereign loveliness,

"Tomorrow we'll let him in," did I respond,

To do the same again tomorrow.

From Friendship with Christ to Contemplation

Jesus wished to establish a close friendship with each of us (see Jn 15:15). We can treat him like a most beloved friend to whom we can confide all our most intimate concerns. No one understands us—or loves us—as he does. He's the ideal friend: He is the only one who loves us with the respect of a best friend and the intense affection of a lover. As St. Josemaría reminds us:

> Jesus is your friend. The Friend. With a human heart, like yours. With loving eyes that wept for Lazarus. And he loves you as much as he loved Lazarus.[39]

We might object that it's not easy to establish a friendship with someone we can't see. But to chat with Jesus, even unseen, is not so difficult if we know him well. We've seen how reading the Gospels and reflecting upon them allows us

---

to get acquainted with his feelings. Moreover, he is always present in every tabernacle, and in daily conversation we learn to recognize his voice in the deepest regions of our soul. We can relate to him just as naturally as to a beloved friend after we've gone blind and half deaf. Despite not being able to see or hear him very well, it's enough to know that he sees and hears us. It's like when a child, far from home, sends his mother a letter. He imagines her reactions as he writes and knows, for example, to avoid mentioning that the food is very bad where he's staying.

We don't see Jesus yet, but he sees us. Although he hides himself so as not to intimidate us, our whole life plays out under his gaze. A sincere gaze can convey all the love we harbor for him. Christ's gaze is always loving, though there are differing "shades" that fluctuate from gratitude and mercy, depending on how we treat him—from the loving look he cast on the rich young man when he told him he kept all the commandments (see Mt 10:20–21) to the merciful gaze that brought tears to Peter's eyes shortly after his denial (see Lk 22:61).

It is easier to grow fond of people who are visible. Still, it's better to have one good, long-distance friend with whom we really "connect" than many neighboring acquaintances who do us favors but are incapable of understanding our inner self. It's a great consolation to have one good friend who can wordlessly grasp all our experiences, even our unspoken thoughts. This is what friendship with Jesus is like. In times of anguish, having such a riend helps us to bear even the most painful solitude. This friendship is not diminished by distance or adversity; in fact, that is when it takes root most firmly. Victor Frankl, recounting his experiences in Auschwitz, explains how during the worst moments of his captivity, he rejoiced simply in thinking of his wife, although he didn't even know whether she was still alive. "I understood how a man who has nothing left in this world still may know bliss, be it only for a brief moment, in the contemplation of his beloved."[40]

With time, friendship with Jesus is transformed into *loving contemplation*, already present but incomplete on earth, consummated in an ineffable and eternal union of love in heaven. Thus Jesus' petition to the Father is answered: "That the love with which thou hast loved me may be in them" (Jn 17:26). Jesus draws us gradually into the highest contemplation of inter-trinitarian life, to this "plenitude of Truth and Love in the mutual contemplation and self-donation (communion) of the Father, Son, and Holy Spirit."[41] The Lord communicates himself to the soul in the intimacy of prayer and offers himself entirely—body, blood, soul, and divinity—in the Eucharist, that "mystery of divine life communicated to human flesh, through the flesh of Christ."[42] The soul opens and the Lord delivers himself up. If the soul responds, this mutual penetration gives rise—even here on earth—to an indescribable bliss, an anticipation of heavenly beatitude. This intimate union of two hearts beating in unison gives us some inkling of the eternal embrace to come in heaven, although here we never lack, as St. John of the Cross puts it, that pain that "naught . . . can cure save the presence and sight of her Beloved."[43]

God does all he can to draw near to us. He not only became man and remains with us in the Eucharist; he has

---

40. Victor Frankl, *Man's Search for Meaning* (New York: Pocket Books, 1985), p. 57.

41. John Paul II, Discourse of May 28, 1986.

42. *The Eucharist: Sacrament of New Life*: official catechetical text for the Great Jubilee of the Year 2000.

43. John of the Cross, *Spiritual Canticle*, in *Spiritual Canticle and Poems* by R. H. J. Stuart, trans. E. Allison Peers (New York: Burns and Oates, 1978), p. 222.

also given us his mother to be ours, thus incorporating us into both his human family (the Holy Family of Nazareth) and his divine family (inter-trinitarian communion). Baptism, by identifying us with Christ, makes us his brothers and sisters, children of God and of Mary. It is fitting for us to draw near to the ineffable divine love by means of his approachable human love. From familiarity with Joseph, Mary, and Jesus, we move on to participate in the divine life where, as sons in the Son, we love the Father in the Holy Spirit. The spiritual life of the Christian begins, then, with a trusting relationship with the "earthly trinity" and moves towards an intimate relationship, in the most sublime contemplation, with each of the Persons of the heavenly Trinity. The holy patriarch, St. Joseph, and his virginal spouse lead us to Jesus, and, holding his hand, we enter into divine intimacy. Trusting interaction with the three members of the family of Nazareth is an intermediate step God has made available to ease our access to him.

One last observation: "It is not possible," says St. Josemaría, "for our poor nature to be so close to God and not to be fired with hunger to sow joy and peace throughout the world."[44] Some, though, are distrustful of the life of prayer, alleging that it lends itself to an individualism that neglects the love of neighbor. Perhaps this may occur in oriental mysticism, but not to the Christian, nor in authentic Christianity; the life of the saints shows that relationship with God fosters love of others. In practice, rather, those who neglect their interior life don't persevere in their altruistic ideals. One young missionary had to return to his native land, exhausted. He acknowledged that his weariness was due to

---

44. Escrivá, *Friends of God*, no. 311.

systematic neglect of his prayer life, and that his veteran companions, being more pious, had been able to continue helping the needy.

There are four reasons why the *vertical dimension* of the Christian life (dealings with God) *strengthens the horizontal dimension* (charity towards one's neighbor). First, God's love purifies our other loves. Second, Christ identifies himself with the happiness of each human being—he's told us that whatever we do for others we do for him (see Mt 25:34–45). If we love him, we'll treat others well, even if they mistreat us. Third, Christ incorporates us into his supernatural family (the Church): Being children of God and of Mary, we know we're brothers and sisters to all the members of this family, living and deceased. And fourth, as we shall see, we are called to be coredeemers with Christ. If we share his zeal for the salvation of souls, none of them will leave us cold, since our coredemptive concern will reach all souls without exception.

COREDEEMERS WITH CHRIST

The paschal mystery, which includes the passion, death, resurrection, ascension, and glorification of Christ, makes up the nucleus of the Christian faith. It's a fascinating mystery that "has changed the course of history, giving to human life an indestructible meaning and value."[45] Indeed, these truths of faith illuminate the deepest meaning of our dignity, our sufferings, and all of our actions. In particular, Christ's passion, by making palpable God's sorrow at our sins, spurs on our generosity as we respond to his love. Let us see first of all how much Christ's redemption dignifies us.

---

45. Benedict XVI, *Easter Sunday homily*, March 23, 2008.

"Man," affirms Pope Benedict, "is worth so much to God that he himself became man in order to *suffer with* man in an utterly real way—in flesh and blood—as is revealed to us in the account of Jesus' Passion."[46] Pointing to our value before God, St. Paul affirms that we have been "bought with a price" (1 Cor 6:20). The word "price" is very interesting for its relationship to other concepts we've employed when speaking of the meaning of one's own dignity—such as the urge to be "valued," the tendency to "overvalue" (arrogance) or "undervalue" oneself (self-rejection), and the desire to be "esteemed" or "appreciated," to be "valued" or "precious" in someone's eyes. In the same way, if someone mistreats us, we might say that they despise us.[47] From this perspective, Christ's passion demonstrates how much he "appreciates" us. The word "redeem," moreover, means to "pay" a ransom—as with a kidnapping, ultimately a measure of the "price" that others are willing to pay in exchange for the prisoner's freedom. If the price amounted to everything someone possessed, no doubt would remain about the esteem in which the redeemer held the hostage. And in fact, the price Christ paid to redeem us was inestimable: his own life, and the shedding of his own blood, down to the last drop. We are worth all the blood of Christ.

The Deepest Love

It's difficult to meditate on Christ's passion "without sharing the emotion that so much sorrow and love arouses."[48]

---

46. Benedict XVI, *Spe salvi*, 39.

47. Translator's note: Spanish *despreciar* (despise), from *precio* (price).

48. A. M. Ramírez, *Meditaciones ante el retablo de Torreciudad* (Pamplona: EUNSA, 2004), p. 119.

The four qualities of ideal love are manifest in it. Let's begin with the *capacity for sacrifice*. "Greater love has no man than this, that a man lay down his life for his friends," says Jesus in John 15:13. One teacher found an effective way of explaining to some children why Jesus had to suffer so much: He asked them how far their parents would be willing to go to find the only medicine that would cure them of chronic pain. They had no doubt, for example, about the trip from Barcelona to Madrid. But their unanimity began to crumble as the distances grew longer: Paris, Moscow, Tokyo. . . . With the help of this anecdote, the instructor concluded that Christ would travel the entire globe to find the medicine.

In his passion, Christ manifests a clear will to suffer the unspeakable, though this was not strictly necessary[49] and he could have avoided it. "He is the freest victim who has ever existed."[50] As a careful reading of the Gospel reveals (see Mt 26:50–54; Jn 19:11), he could have curtailed his agony and died sooner, just as he rose when he wished. "I lay down my life," he had said, "that I may take it up again. No one takes it from me, but I lay it down of my own accord. I have power to lay it down, and I have power to take it again" (Jn 10:17–18). The centurion's surprise at Jesus' active manner of expiring (see Lk 23:46–47; Mk 15:39) is no wonder: The usual course of a man losing that much blood would be first, a loss of consciousness, then a state of shock, followed by death. This happened with all victims of crucifixion. Jesus, on the other hand, never lost consciousness for a moment. He gave up his spirit

---

49. With respect to simple justice, in order to pay our debt, such a painful passion was not necessary. Given the infinite, divine dignity of the Word made flesh, a minimal sacrifice would have sufficed to make reparation to the Father for our sins.

50. Urbano, *La madre*, p. 18.

after three long hours on the cross, right after pronouncing his last words, and at the precise instant at which he was on the point of fainting. He could have suffered less, dying sooner, but he didn't choose to.

Why did Jesus choose to suffer so much if it wasn't strictly necessary and could have been avoided? Although it was not required, it was fitting: In this was the will of the Father, with which Christ lovingly complied. But then another question arises: Why did the Father arrange things so that his Son would suffer so greatly? Bl. John Paul II explains: "Without the suffering and death of Christ, God's love for men would not have been manifest in all its depth and greatness."[51] In the end, the Passion was the most suitable way for both Jesus and God the Father to manifest the depth and refinement of their love. "Both suffer. And both subject themselves to the whims of human freedom."[52] Christ's love and sorrow reveal to us in an accessible way the Father's love and sorrow. On the cross, undergoing maximum suffering and loving us to the end, he reveals the intensity of divine love, just as his own imaginable human sorrow reveals the ineffable pain of God.

A twofold motive for love—for us and for the Father—inspires Christ's passion. As our brother, he suffers not only to redeem us, but also to console God the Father for the pain our sins inflict upon him. There is also a twofold reason that it was fitting for Jesus to have made the greatest sacrifice: with respect to us, to give us unmistakable certainty of his affection; with respect to his Father, that the satisfaction might be proportionate to the magnitude of his sorrow. Seeing how

---

51. John Paul II, address, October 19, 1998.
52. Urbano, *La madre*, p. 70.

much Jesus suffered, we comprehend the extent of his love for us and of the love needed to console the Father.

Apart from his capacity for sacrifice, the Passion manifests another quality of ideal love: its *respect for freedom*. This is another aspect of divine love that Jesus reveals to us. Meditating on the Gospels, one is struck by how, from the time Jesus is taken prisoner, he endures continual insults and blows but does not defend himself in the least. Christ suffers as a man but does not cease to be God, so that those who torture him as a man are in fact torturing God. Thus, in Christ, God himself is insulted without making a move to resist his torturers. Isaiah prophesied this when he spoke of the lamb led to the slaughter, this man of sorrows who does not turn his face before "shame and spitting" (Is. 50:6). This was the "script" agreed upon by Jesus and his Father so that we would grasp the vulnerability of a God who loves us and delicately respects our freedom.

Let's look at the other two qualities of an ideal love: *purity of intention* and *interior freedom*. The first couldn't be greater than in such a disinterested sacrifice: Christ is innocent and thinks only of consoling his Father and winning our happiness. The second is found in the very essence of his delivering himself up right to the end. Here is where he shows us what *freedom of love* looks like: a glad and limitless self-giving. Jesus embraced the cross because "he was loving even more than he was suffering."[53] If it is meritorious to be willing to suffer for the beloved's good, it's much more so to do it with joy. Only a great love makes this possible. The more the desire to make someone happy drives us onward, the easier it is for joy to overcome pain. Our Lord Jesus Christ, incomprehensible as it

---

53. Escrivá, *Way of the Cross*, 12th Station, no. 3.

may seem, loved so much that, as he was suffering the cruelest of torments, he experienced an immense inner happiness.

The Christian Meaning of Suffering

The Passion also offers us a magnificent context for contemplating the depravity of sin, inasmuch as it proves the terrible ingratitude of our coldness. After the Passion, every sin is more repulsive. It's as if we gave a kidney to save the life of a brother in need of dialysis only to have him refuse us an insignificant sacrifice: the rejection would be much more painful. "What," wonders Thibon, "must the pain of God, who loves us madly, be like? And to know, my God, that I am necessary to you in your infinite riches, as the beloved to the lover, and that you agonize little by little under the infinite weight of the love I deny you?"[54]

In light of this reflection, we can understand better how our sins increase the weight of Christ's cross, and also how we can lighten his burden, uniting ourselves in love to his redemptive sacrifice.[55] Here is the key for deepening our understanding of the Christian meaning of suffering, both voluntary

---

54. Thibon, *Nuestra mirada ciega ante la luz*, p. 167.

55. The classical explanation of the sufferings of Christ rests on all his actions—since he is true God—transcending the limits of time and space. Given that "[a]ll that Christ is—all that he did and suffered for all men—participates in the divine eternity" (*CCC*, 1085), we can, two thousand years later, truly modify the weight of his cross. In this regard, when addressing the Sacred Heart, the *Catechism* says: "Jesus knew and loved us each and all during his life, his agony, and his Passion and gave himself up for each one of us" (478).

In any case, without entering into theological minutiae, I venture to believe that the actuality of Christ's passion is not simply the consequence of his divine nature, but can also be explained in terms of his human nature. Given that Christ's sacred humanity is contemplating us from heaven, it is not strange to think that all (mortification) and involuntary (adversities). For a Christian, suffering is not only an occasion of purification, a chance to mature within, as when a serious illness can help someone to "discern in his life what is not essential so that he can turn towards what is."[56] Jesus goes much further: He teaches us to transform suffering into a love with eternal repercussions. But first of all, to maintain order in our discussion, we must address the origin of evil and suffering in the world, a mystery that transcends our understanding—although Christ's passion offers a modicum of light.

According to Sacred Scripture, evil appears in the world because of sin. God does not desire our suffering, but he permits it out of respect for our freedom. We have every indication that if God decided to create us, knowing that we would introduce evil into the world, it must have been because he had a plan of redemption to set right what was twisted, liberating us from sin through Christ's passion. The grace he obtained for us on the cross enables us to conquer evil, following his example. "Each one is also *called to share in that suffering* through which the Redemption was accomplished,"[57]

---

the good and evil here on earth resounds in that glorious heart which "loves continually the eternal Father and all men." (Pius XII, *Haurietis aguas* in Denzinger, no. 3924). Sacred Scripture indeed confirms that Jesus Christ identifies affectively with us here on earth. Thus he affirmed that he would remain with us until the end of the age (see Mt 28:20) and that whatever we might do to one another, we would do to him (see Mt 25:34–35). When, after the ascension, he appears to Saul on the road to Damascus, he asks him "Why do you persecute me?" (Acts 9:4; see also 22:7–8). St Augustine, commenting on these passages, states that Jesus, despite having been "raised to the heights of heaven" as Head of the mystical body that is the Church, "he continues to suffer on earth through the fatigues that his members experience" (Sermon on the Ascension of the Lord, 98, 1–2).

56. *CCC*, 1501.

57. John Paul II, *Salvifici doloris*, no. 19.

but—since God doesn't impose his will on us—it depends on our individual acceptance or rejection of the invitation to unite ourselves to that redemptive sacrifice. The chance to ease Christ's pain and help him save souls opens up unsuspected horizons for us. St. Faustina recounts the Lord telling her: "I am giving you a share in the redemption of mankind. You are solace in my dying hour."[58] If we unite ourselves to the redemptive sacrifice out of love of God and souls, our sorrow can be turned to joy. "What does suffering matter if we suffer to console, to please God our Lord, in a spirit of reparation, united to him on his Cross: in a word, if we suffer for Love?"[59]

To deepen our sense of the mystery of the Christian meaning of suffering, we have, besides revelation, the help of the "*lived theology* of the saints."[60] They are the ones who teach us, with their doctrine and their lives, what Edith Stein called the "science of the cross."[61] The sorrow of the saints is turned to joy, for they know they are alleviating the pain of the one they love most. They don't merely accept and love the cross; in their madness of love, they desire it ardently. This is illustrated by the examples of St. Margaret Mary Alacoque and St. Josemaría. The former, a "connoisseur" of the heart of Jesus, affirms: "There is nothing that attracts me so much as the Cross; I suffer so little, that my greatest suffering consists

---

58. *Diary of St. Faustina: Divine Mercy in My Soul* (Stockbridge, Mass.: Marian Press, 1987), no. 310. (See pdf at *http://www.basilica.org/pages/ebooks/St.%20 Faustina-Divine%20Mercy%20in%20my%20Soul.pdf.*)

59. Escrivá, *The Way*, no. 182.

60. John Paul II, *Tertio millenio ineunte*, no. 27.

61. See Edith Stein, *The Science of the Cross: The Collected Works of Edith Stein VI* (Washington: ICS Publications, 2003).

of not suffering enough."[62] St. Josemaría was thirty years old when he told the Lord:

> Jesus, I feel so much desire to make reparation. My path is to love and to suffer. But love makes me rejoice in the suffering, so that now it seems impossible for me ever to suffer. I've told you already: there's no one who can upset me. And I would still add: there's no one who can make me suffer, because suffering gives me joy and peace.[63]

The saints have understood that the sorrow of the redeemed is a coredemptive sorrow.

Coredemption

The mystery of suffering, then, is tied to another great mystery: coredemption with Christ. Only he can mediate between God and man, but he wishes us to be associated with his redemptive sacrifice.[64] As good "Cyrenes," if we carry his cross, we help him to bear it. Identifying ourselves with him, sharing his sufferings (see 1 Pt 3:14), we participate actively in the work of the Redemption, becoming "another Christ"— "Christ himself" (see Gal 2:19–20; Rom 6:4 and Phil 2:5). In this sense, St. Paul says, "I have been crucified with Christ"

---

62. In J. Croiset, *The Devotion to the Sacred Heart of Jesus* (Rockford, Ill.: Tan Books, 2003), pp. 13–14.

63. In A. Vásquez de Prada, *El Fundador del Opus Dei, I: ¡Señor, que vea!*, 8th ed. (Madrid: Rialp, 2004), pp. 418–419.

64. To avoid misunderstanding, the Second Vatican Council, instead of speaking of "coredemption," preferred to employ the terms "participation" and "cooperation." "[N]o creature could ever be counted as equal with the Incarnate Word and Redeemer. Just as the priesthood of Christ is shared in various ways . . . so also the unique mediation of the Redeemer does not exclude but rather gives rise to a manifold cooperation which is but a sharing in this one source" (*Lumen gentium*, no. 62).

(Gal 2:20), and "in my flesh I complete what is lacking in Christ's afflictions" (Col 1:24). Bl. John Paul II explains this mysterious reality:

> In this dimension—the dimension of love—the Redemption which has already been completely accomplished is, in a certain sense, constantly being accomplished. . . . Faith in sharing the suffering of Christ brings with it the interior certainty that the suffering person "completes what is lacking in Christ's afflictions," the certainty that in the spiritual dimension of the work of Redemption *he is serving*, like Christ, *the salvation of his brothers and sisters.*[65]

We might say that one of Jesus' five wounds, the one in his side, is still not healed. Coldness wounds his heart; love gives it solace. With this sorrow of love, Jesus redeems us, and our acts of love console his wounded heart. We suffer with his sorrow, but it consoles us to mitigate it for him. It is instructive to see what happened to St. Faustina when the Lord allowed her to contemplate his scourging. "My heart almost stopped at the sight of these tortures. The Lord said to me, 'I suffer even greater pain than that which you see. . . . Look and see the human race in its present condition.'" Faustina, having seen in detail the sins of so many, was left disconsolate. "Then the Lord said to me, 'I see the sincere pain of your heart which brought great solace to my heart. See and take comfort.'"[66]

"Jesus will be in agony until the end of the world: one must not fall asleep during all that time," wrote Pascal.[67] Just

---

65. John Paul II, *Salvifici doloris*, nos. 24 and 27.

66. M. F. Kowalska, *Diario: La Divina Misericordia en mi alma* (Granada: Levántate, 2003), no. 445.

67. B. Pascal, *Pensées*, no. 553

as God wanted an angel to comfort Jesus in the Garden of Olives, "even now, in a wondrous yet true manner, we can and ought to console the Most Sacred Heart which is continually wounded by the sins of thankless men."[68] As St. Thérèse says, "Our little love dries the tears that the evil ones cause him to shed."[69] The saints perceive these realities because their love for Christ arouses in them "a longing to understand his tears, to see his smile, his face . . ."[70] Thus, like St. Thérèse, they suffer when they see that "from the worldly," Jesus "meets only with ingratitude and indifference, and even among His disciples, there are very few who surrender fully to the tenderness of His infinite love."[71] The holy Frenchwoman, to make up for so much cold indifference, "when she was gravely ill, in her moments of greatest suffering, when she could no longer speak, took the crucifix in her hands and with her fingers made as if to pull the nails from Jesus Christ's hands and feet."[72]

"Powerful is suffering when it is as voluntary as sin," declares Paul Claudel.[73] Our little crosses acquire an enormous dignity since they are *transformed into the very cross of Christ.* As long as we carry them, he need not. Light as our crosses may be compared with his, they do not therefore fail to participate in the unique, redemptive cross. If someone gave us a *lignum crucis* (relic of the Cross), even if it were only a tiny

68. Pius XI, *Miserentissimus Redemptor*, May 9, 1928, no. 13 [Spanish edition incorrectly says no. 17].

69. Thérèse of Lisieux, in Manglano, *Orar con Teresa de Lisieux*, p. 67.

70. Escrivá, *Friends of God*, no. 310.

71. Thérèse of Lisieux, *The Autobiography of St. Thérèse: Story of a Soul* (New York: Image/Doubleday, 2001), p. 157.

72. T. Dajczer, *Meditaciones sobre la fe* (Madrid: San Pablo, 1994), p. 238.

73. Paul Claudel, *The Tidings Brought to Mary* (Connecticut: Yale University Press, 1916), p. 107.

splinter, we would possess something of the highest value. Thus, every time the Lord asks a sacrifice of us or allows us to pass through a tribulation, he is inviting us to carry his cross. "Our Lord, with his arms outstretched, is continually begging for your love," affirms St. Josemaría, contemplating the crucifix.[74] These "alms" are not obligatory, but if we know Christ's pain we can no longer remain indifferent. And if we truly love him, once we know that our crosses alleviate his suffering, our sorrow is turned to joy. So it was for one holy woman dying of intestinal tuberculosis. In the midst of her intense pain, she wrote, "How blessed . . . to be able to console the Agonizing Heart of our Jesus with little acts of love!"[75]

Reflecting upon the "terrible ingratitude of the human heart," we understand "why the Cross of Jesus weighs so much."[76] Being in tune with the pain that our sins provoke in him is an incentive to foster the *spirit of reparation*. If our mother were ill, the happiness our visits brought her would lead us to exert ourselves to visit. But if our brothers and sisters never came to see her, we would feel the urgency of being with her even more. We wouldn't be able to prevent the pain their absence caused her, but our affection would at least serve as a balm. Analogously, the love of Christ urges us (see 2 Cor 5:14) to make amends to him, for not a day goes by when he doesn't suffer outrages, indifference, and ingratitude that wounds his heart. "You must realize," recalls St. Josemaría, "that Jesus is being offended constantly, and unfortunately, these offences are not being atoned for at the same rate."[77]

---

74. Escrivá, *The Forge*, no. 404.

75. In J. M. Cejas, *María Ignacia García Escobar en los comienzos del Opus Dei* (Madrid: Rialp, 2001), p. 179.

76. Escrivá, *Way of the Cross*, 3rd Station.

77. Escrivá, *Furrow*, no. 480.

There are so many reasons for compassion that perhaps we feel a certain "vertigo" when we try to imagine Jesus' sorrow. To get an idea of the magnitude of his heart's suffering, it's enough to think of the great number of people who are unresponsive to him, or the many daily Masses celebrated or attended with cold indifference (Jesus' vulnerability is at its height in the Eucharist, for it is there where he loves most). The awareness of the overwhelming weight of our sins enkindles in us a desire to lighten his burden. St. Faustina tells how one day the Lord said to her, "My daughter, I want to repose in your heart, because many souls have thrown me out of their hearts today. I have experienced sorrow unto death."[78] We know that Jesus is not exaggerating about his pain— just the opposite. It is to be hoped he will not say, like the psalmist, "Insults have broken my heart, so that I am in despair; I looked for pity, but there was none; and for comforters, but I found none . . ." (Ps 69:20).

To coredeem with Christ is not simply to lighten his cross; it also entails a relationship with God the Father and with all people. By redeeming us, Jesus reconciled us to the Father and opened the gates of heaven. Being coredeemers with him, we help him console God the Father and save souls. Let's take a moment to reflect on the *reparation* that we offer to the Father, which includes consolation and reparation for our own trespasses. We not only contribute to mitigating the sadness that our lack of love inflicts on him, but we also move towards making good on our debt. The realm of love does not exclude that of justice. As we shall see, human malice deserves a punishment that would repair the injustice. Thus, Christ, the only innocent party, at once consoles the Father

---

78. Kowalska, *Diary*, no. 866.

and helps us to pay all our debts. As coredeemers, we help him not only console the Father, but *expiate* all the sins of history. St. Bernard calls it "vicarious satisfaction." He makes reparation in our stead, and we can help him. In any case, God is not only the guarantor of justice, but also the chief offended party. Thus, reparation, beyond a mere satisfaction of justice, consists above all of loving reparation.

Let us focus now on the relation between coredemption and the *salvation of souls*. It's only natural to wish for everyone to share in our happiness. I don't mean simply the concern for drawing others to God through good example and advice, but also collaborating with Christ by obtaining the graces they need. Apostolic activity is only fruitful to the degree that it is joined to redemptive sacrifice. Only the Holy Spirit can move hearts, and the outpouring of that Spirit is the fruit of the cross. It is not only those who happen to be close by who benefit from zeal for souls. Through the communion of saints, God has established a kind of solidarity among us all, so that, breaking barriers of time and space, we can help even those we don't know. If we share in Christ's eagerness to redeem, we will feel driven to help him save every person on the way to heaven. With this aim, we offer prayers and sacrifices, especially for *sinners in their last agony* who will be condemned unless they convert.

The realism of numbers may help us grasp what is at stake. According to statistics published in 2007, each year, eighty-six people out of every 10,000 die. On the Internet, these numbers are updated every second.[79] As I write, the earth has 6,871,706,632 inhabitants. Rounding off, I calculate that every year 53,000,000 people die; every week

---

79. See the World Clock at *www.poodwaddle.com*.

1,000,000; every day 150,000; every hour 6,000; every minute 100. These are numbers that give us pause.[80] If we're in tune with Christ's thirst for redemption, we won't be indifferent to a single one of these souls. It's good to keep in mind the 150,000 a day because, as we shall see, each day in the Holy Mass, all our redemptive desires can converge.

The Holy Mass

Coredemption is closely linked to the Eucharist. In the Mass, "time blends with eternity,"[81] since it is there that the paschal mystery is renewed—in an unbloody but real manner (the redemptive sacrifice, the resurrection, and the glorification of Christ). By virtue of this "perennial making present of the paschal mystery," there comes about a "mysterious oneness in time" between something that happened two thousand years ago and "the passage of the centuries."[82] As the *Catechism* summarizes it, this is the "unique event of history which does not pass away. . . . His Paschal mystery is a real event that occurred in our history, but it is unique: all other historical events happen once, and then pass away, swallowed up in the past. . . . The event of the Cross and Resurrection abide."[83] As the liturgy affirms, Jesus "does not cease to offer himself for us."[84] Pope Benedict XVI echoes this same idea through St. Peter Julian Eymard: "The Holy Eucharist is Jesus Christ past, present, and future."[85]

---

80. Escrivá, *Furrow*, no. 897.

81. Escrivá, *Christ Is Passing By*, no. 94.

82. John Paul II, *Ecclesia de Eucharistia*, no. 5.

83. *CCC*, 1085.

84. Roman Missal, Paschal Preface no. 3.

85. Benedict XVI, September 14, 2008 address at the Sanctuary of Lourdes (on Eucharistic Adoration).

Participation in the Eucharistic sacrifice allows us, therefore, to make a leap in time and space. It is like being at Golgotha, in the present moment, and in heaven, witnessing all the joys and all the redemptive sufferings of Christ. Thus the final words of the consecration: "Do this in memory of me," with which Jesus instituted two sacraments, the Eucharist and holy orders. The word "memory" (or "commemoration"), Bl. John Paul II clarifies, does not mean "a symbolic evocation of the past, but the living presence of the Lord in the midst of his own."[86] Here we are speaking of a "memorial in the biblical sense, a memorial which *makes present* the event itself. It is *memory* and *presence*."[87] It is a great help during Mass to consider that the Eucharist, far from being the symbolic representation of a past event, is a sacrifice that is still being offered in a mysterious yet real manner. We would do well to recall, and to live what we are seeing, with the eyes of our souls: the most important events of the Christ's redemption and glorification. It's not like watching a play or a movie or a "prerecorded program." Attending Mass is equivalent to witnessing "live" all the redemptive sorrows and joys of Christ.

It would be a shame merely to be a passive spectator as the redemptive sacrifice is renewed. In the consecration of the wine, after the "take," which indicates a delicate entreaty to accept his loving surrender, Jesus Christ says to us, "and drink from it, for this is the chalice of my blood." These words contain a veiled invitation not to leave him alone: to respond to him by our coredemption. Among the Jews, to drink from the chalice meant to share actively in the sacrifice (see 1 Cor 10:16–33). This is why Jesus would have asked the sons of

---

86. John Paul II, Letter to Priests for Holy Thursday, 2000.
87. John Paul II, *Gift and Mystery* (New York: Image/Doubleday), p. 76.

Zebedee if they were ready to drink of the chalice from which he was going to drink (see Mt 20:22).[88] He was referring to the chalice of the "new and eternal covenant" between God and men, sealed with his blood and "poured out," as the words of consecration continue, "for you and for many for the forgiveness of sins."

Between the "you" and the "many" stretches a duration of centuries. In the Eucharistic celebration, all Christ's desires for all people of all eras converge. Jesus is immolated "in forgiving of the sins we commit each day"[89]—the sins of all those in attendance at the liturgy as well as all those absent. Each Mass is identical but numerically distinct. All the blessed and all the souls in purgatory, but only a portion of us who are still on the way, share in the sacrifice. Every Eucharist has an incalculable value, but it is applied each time to the benefit of different people. We renew daily the same paschal mystery, awaiting the second coming of Christ at the end of time. And there we can join daily, together with Mary, with all the redemptive sufferings of her Son, the physical pains of his passion as well as the moral ones for our sins. In some sense, each sin is redeemed with a corresponding pain.

A Priestly Soul

If we unite ourselves to the redemptive sacrifice in the Mass with a priestly soul, we participate in the most remarkable undertaking in the history of humanity. All of our daily actions, even the most prosaic, placed on the altar take on an extraordinary transcendence. As St. Josemaría teaches, to

---

88. To respond to the Lord's love, says Ps 116, "I will lift up the cup of salvation."
89. Paul VI, *Mysterium fidei*, no. 27.

live ordinary life in a holy way entails, as in the story of King Midas, transforming everything we touch into "supernatural gold."[90] In the midst of our toil and busyness, adding love to the duties of each moment, we help to "unite all things in [Christ]" (Eph 1:10). We lighten his cross, contribute to the consolation of God the Father, and obtain the gift of the Holy Spirit for the salvation of souls. These three coredemptive elements appear at the end of every Eucharistic prayer: "Through him, with him, and in him." This contains a whole guide for living. In every Eucharistic celebration, the Church makes an offering to Christ and also offers herself with him. Thus, by "placing on the paten" our efforts at improvement, besides offering some sacrifice "for him," we offer ourselves "with him" to the Father in reparation for sins, and also "in him" we beg the Holy Spirit for the salvation of those on earth and in purgatory. Thus we have a threefold cause for love: love of Christ, love of God the Father, and—through the Holy Spirit—love of our fellow creatures.

Thus, a whole panorama opens up for our efforts, motivated by the desire to alleviate the pain of Christ's heart "frequently, daily."[91] Lukewarmness is incompatible with the pressing urgency to coredeem with him. "A priestly heart that does not *bleed* is no priestly heart at all," said one Belgian saint.[92] Moreover, if we really love the Lord, the chance to lighten his cross allows us to endure any hardship. "For You,

90. Escrivá, *Friends of God*, no. 308.

91. Escrivá, *Forge*, no. 442.

92. In Em. R. De Roover, *Priester Poppe. Leven en zending* (Altiora: Averbode, 1987), p. 17. Edward Poppe (1890–1924) was a Flemish priest beatified by John Paul II on October 3, 1999.

Jesus, I would be crucified if it could prevent your sufferings," said one young poet.[93] Before the crucifix, another exclaimed:

> Body wounded by love,
> I adore you and I follow you,
> Lord of Lords, I
> Want to share your sorrows
> Mounting the Cross with you.[94]

"Love makes suffering fruitful and suffering deepens love," declares Bl. John Paul II.[95] There are two main ways of coming to love someone deeply: *gratitude* for his goodness and *compassion* upon seeing him suffer. Meditating on Jesus' passion and sensing palpably his love and pain can also inspire affection in us. This is the best spur to our generosity in everyday sacrifice. Self-donation tends to be preceded by compassion. If good parents love their children so much, perhaps it is because of the many years of taking compassion on their neediness and sacrificing themselves for them. If we witness a serious traffic accident and see that the driver, a perfect stranger, lies bleeding on the street, we feel a need to help him. How much more will we have compassion on the redemptive sufferings of our brother and best friend?

The heart of Jesus is not the only one to suffer the sorrow of love. Mary's heart also has shared that sorrow for twenty centuries. As Benedict XVI points out, she "accepted, two thousand years ago, to give everything, to offer her body so

---

93. B. Llorens, in J. I. Poveda, *Bartlomé. Una sed de eternidades* (Madrid: Rialp, 1997), p. 138.

94. J. M. Pemán, *Ante el Cristo de la buena muerte*, in *Pasión según Pemán* (Madrid: Edibesa, 1997), p. 87.

95. John Paul II, Homily, October 11, 1998, Canonization of Edith Stein.

as to receive the Body of the Creator. Everything came from Christ, even Mary; everything came through Mary, even Christ."[96] Their hearts beat in unison. Both have a glorified body, and from heaven they contemplate, in a vigil of love, all the good and evil that we do. They will not be "at rest" until after the Second Coming, when this world has ended and there is nobody still on the road to heaven.

Nobody lightens Jesus' cross so much as his mother. This is why she wanted to stay so close during the Crucifixion. This was the divine plan for her, long contemplated, announced when the aged Simeon prophesied that a sword would pierce her heart (see Lk 2:35). Only she understood fully why it was fitting for her son to be sacrificed. The apostles, though taught by him, didn't understand it, whereas she, with her priestly soul, had three reasons for wanting to remain at the foot of the cross: to sustain her son, to offer consolation with him to the Father, and, in him, to obtain saving grace. Ever since she agreed to associate herself to that redeeming sacrifice, she became our mother. When Jesus offered her to us in the person of John (see Jn 19:26–27), he didn't *make* her a mother: he simply *declared* it. Mary, the coredemptrix *par excellence*,[97] "shar[es] her Son's compassion for sinners."[98] Thus, so many times, she urges us to console the Lord and to pray for sinners. From her we learn to turn our entire "existence into a coredemption of Love."[99]

---

96. Benedict XVI, Discourse of September 14, 2008, at the Sanctuary of Lourdes.

97. To avoid misunderstandings, the Second Vatican Council recalls that the titles by which the Church invokes Mary—Advocate, Auxiliatrix, Adjutrix, and Mediatrix— are to be so understood that they neither take away from nor add anything to the dignity and efficaciousness of Christ the one Mediator (see *Lumen gentium*, no. 62).

98. Benedict XVI, Homily of September 15, 2008, in the Sanctuary of Lourdes.

99. Escrivá, *Furrow*, no. 255.

6.

Merciful Love

A deep love requires us to come out of ourselves, forget our own needs, and focus on those of others. Love leads us to be attentive: It involves being attuned to the beloved. We succeed in this to the degree that we overcome self-centeredness and discover what others' needs are—decreasing centripetal and increasing centrifugal force. God's love fosters both aspects. On the one hand, we have confirmed that Christ's passion facilitates this living outside ourselves, since the open wound of his heart, as St. Bernard puts it, cries out for attention and relief.[1] On the other hand, nothing promotes self-forgetfulness so much as the reconciliation to one's own wretchedness that God's merciful love makes possible.

This facet of God's love is closely related to divine filiation, and at the same time it serves as a guarantee of inner peace. Knowing ourselves to be children of a merciful Father is incompatible with being overwhelmed by our faults. From this perspective, we understand better the extent to which our sins pain the Lord—but also his immense joy whenever we

---

1. See Bernard de Clairvaux, *In Cantica Canticorum*, Sermon 83, 4. "*Clamat vulrus!*" ("The wound cries out!"), exclaims the saint.

return, contrite and trusting, to the tribunal of divine mercy. We share both his sorrow for sin and his joy at reconciliation. We promise to amend our lives, and every time we don't manage it, we return to the house of our Father with the joy of knowing that "nothing pleases him more than our coming back to him with true repentance."[2]

THE TRIBUNAL OF MERCY

We should be very grateful for the sacrament of reconciliation. "It is wonderful to be able to confess our sins, and to hear as a balm the word which floods us with mercy and sends us on our way again."[3] If someone isn't inclined to rejoice after confession, it may be because he hasn't forgiven himself, or because he isn't aware of the joy his repentance gives the Father. God doesn't love sin, but he loves the sinner. Recall the tenderness of the father in the parable, embracing his prodigal son: "He ran and embraced him," it says, "and kissed him" (Lk 15:20) Moreover, he doesn't offer us this glad forgiveness only once. If we're contrite, he forgives us for the same fault with the same joy a thousand times a day. The sacrament of confession and acts of contrition—"with which even lost battles are not lost"[4]—restores peace to the soul. Every time we beg forgiveness, we can exclaim, in the words of the Easter liturgy: *Felix culpa* (*Happy fault*)!

What we feel upon reconciling with the people we love can help us imagine the Lord's joy when we ask his pardon. St.

---

2. Maximus the Confessor, Letter 11: from the Office of Readings for Wednesday of the 4th week of Lent.

3. John Paul II, *Letter to Priests*, March 25, 2001, no. 10.

4. Urbano, p. 288.

Thérèse said to a nun who asked her forgiveness, "Never have I felt so strongly the love with which Jesus receives us when we ask forgiveness after having offended him. If I, poor creature, have felt such love for you when you have come to me, what will happen in the heart of the good God when we return to him?"[5] Repentance is always a proof of love. One lady understood this through an experience of mixed feelings toward her absentminded and unpunctual husband. On one occasion, as on so many others, it had done no good for her to insist with all earnestness the need for him to arrive by a certain time for an important appointment. Her husband arrived late yet again, but this time with a bouquet of flowers for her. Her initial reaction was anger, but when she reflected a bit more on his gesture, she perceived the close connection between repentance, forgiveness, and the depth of love. She understood then that God's love is so perfect that our contrition means much more to him than all the flowers in the world.

WHAT DOES IT MEAN TO BE MERCIFUL?

The Bible speaks of God as compassionate and merciful over 300 times. Mercy means not only indulgence, but also a predilection for the neediest and a heartfelt identification with them. We see this quality in loving mothers. "If I were a leper my mother would hug me. She would kiss my wounds without fear or hesitation."[6] This is why the Old Testament uses the word *rahamim*, meaning "womb," to express the ideas that God has inner depths of mercy. "God is maternally paternal,"

5. In M.-D. Poinsenet, *Thérèse de Lisieux, témoin de la foi* (Tours: Mama, 1969), p. 351.
6. Escrivá, *The Forge*, no. 190.

said St. Francis de Sales. Mercy proceeds from the love God has for us because he loves us like a mother with a special affection for her weakest child.

The Gospel tells us that "when [Jesus] saw the crowds, he had compassion for them, because they were harassed and helpless, like sheep without a shepherd" (Mt 9:36). The expression "had compassion" can be misunderstood. In some languages, it has lost its original meaning and is equivalent to "had pity," with a connotation of humiliation or even contempt. To "have compassion" on someone has come to mean informing him with an air of superiority that we will help him despite how little we love him. Thus, to *love out of compassion* is to *love out of obligation*. However, the word comes from the Latin *compatire*, meaning to *suffer together* with someone, to share another's unhappiness; indeed, to accompany him in this sentiment is impossible without an emotional identification. In some languages, the term retains broader and more positive connotations, as with the German *mitgefühl*, which means to share any kind of sentiment: joy or pain, happiness or anguish. In any case, there can no doubt that, in the hierarchy of sentiments, compassion is one of the noblest.

His mercy doesn't lead Christ to look down on us, but rather to feel as his own all that concerns us, to identify himself with our joys and sorrows, and even to love us more than we love ourselves. "Lord, have mercy on me, a sinner," we pray, imploring his mercy. The depths of Christ's merciful heart is similar to what we see in the best of mothers. Thus, we should go to confession with the same disposition we would have in asking forgiveness of a good mother who suffers in silence because of our caprice. Christ's mercy is perhaps the most moving facet of his love. His generosity in his passion is certainly astonishing, but with his mercy we sense a more "personalized" love. Nailed to the cross, he loves us *individually*: He suffers for love of us all, although he would endure this death if any of us were the only one. By contrast, the depths of his mercy make us feel loved in an "exceptional" way: He has compassion on us all, but he takes into account the uniqueness of each of us. He is like a mother who adapts her love to the peculiarities of each of her sons or daughters.

These two sources of Christ's love are related: generosity passes by way of mercy. We see it in every heart that has compassion on another's wretchedness, feeling it as its own and thus ready to serve in any way possible. "Do you not know," asked St. Augustine, "that to have mercy means to make oneself wretched, to feel the pain of the other?"[7] The term *misericordia* comes from *miseria* ("misery") and *cor* ("heart"). As St. Thomas Aquinas explains, "A person is said to be merciful as being, so to speak, sorrowful at heart [*miserum cor*]; being affected with sorrow at the misery of another as though it were his own. Hence it follows that he endeavors to dispel the misery of this other."[8]

All that God has done for us is a consequence of this affective identification that every merciful lover harbors. We think, for instance, of the Incarnation, which enabled the Word to share our wretched human condition. "Is there anything," asked St. Bernard, "that could declare his mercy more unequivocally than his having accepted our misery?"[9] The Redemption, too, has its roots in a God who is "rich in mercy" (Eph 2:4) His merciful heart has driven him, in Christ, to give his life to free us from the wretchedness of our

---

7. Augustine, *De moribus* 1, 28, 56.
8. Aquinas, *Summa Theologiae*, I, q. 21, a. 3.
9. Bernard de Clairvaux, *Sermon 1 on the Epiphany of the Lord*, 1–2, *Patrologia latina*, 143.

sin. As Pope Benedict XVI affirms, "The cross is truly the place where God's compassion for our world is perfectly manifested."[10] The love "that descends to the very center of evil to conquer it with good"[11] inspired the saving plan of the Father through the cross of his Son. Jesus explained it to Nicodemus when he told him, "For God so loved the world that he gave his only Son, that whoever believes in him should not perish but have eternal life" (Jn 3:16).

In God, omnipotence is at the service of mercy. By contrast, in cultures not inspired by Christianity, compassion denotes weakness, cowardice, and dishonor.[12] The fact is, though, that humbly offering and accepting forgiveness requires great bravery. Moreover, mercy helps to resolve many disputes, and without reconciliation there is no peace, either between persons or nations. Bl. John Paul II emphasized this when he said, "The daily experiences of human life show very clearly how much forgiveness and reconciliation are indispensable if there is to be genuine renewal, both personal and social."[13]

MERCIFUL HEART

Christ also reveals to us the depths of the Father's mercy. As Pope Benedict XVI affirms, Christ's predilection for the most needy is "the central nucleus of the gospel message."[14] Christ reproached the Pharisees for their intolerance for sinners,

---

10. Benedict XVI, Homily of September 15, 2008.

11. John Paul II, Address of July 27, 1986, no. 2. See also address of May 29, 1999, no. 3.

12. See John Paul II, *Dives in misericordia*, no. 2. See also homily of March 25, 1998.

13. John Paul II, Message for Lent, 2001, no. 2.

14. Benedict XVI, Address of March 30, 2008 (2nd Sunday of Easter).

saying: "Those who are well have no need of a physician, but those who are sick. Go and learn what this means: 'I desire mercy, and not sacrifice.' For I came not to call the righteous, but sinners" (Mt 9:12–13). The Lord urges us to acknowledge our needs humbly so that he may satisfy them. Thus, he insists that we become like little children (see Mt 18:1–4; Mk 10:14; Lk 18:15–17; 9:46–48). Children, in their simplicity, recognize their weakness and allow themselves to be loved. Knowing that Christ has compassion on our wretchedness helps us to acknowledge it ourselves and to purify our intention when we ask forgiveness. If we sympathize with the pain we're causing him, we will feel compassion for him as well as a sense of urgency to ease his pain by asking for his pardon.

It helps us to evoke the merciful glance of Christ, the same one he directed at Levi, at Zacchaeus, at the woman taken in adultery, at the Samaritan woman, and especially at Peter (see Mt 18:1–4; Mk 10:14; Lk 18:15–17; 9:46–48). Although it's impossible to capture in a painting Jesus' expression after the threefold denial of his disciple-friend, it's worth trying to imagine it. When we sin, our tendency to project our lack of indulgence onto Jesus makes us miss out on understanding his true self. We don't dare look him in the eye, imagining that he is staring at us with a severe expression. We forget that he never distances himself from us, though we may try to avoid him. This is why it's good to engrave on our memory that merciful glance which, far from accusing, is above all an expression of love that invites us to reconciliation. It's a mixture of tender compassion and loving reproach; it encapsulates, at the same time and for the same loving reason, the pain of the offense and the desire to make peace—the pain that seeks to hide itself and the hope of a happy outcome. That merciful glance of Jesus is irresistible; when Peter saw it in the high priest's house, "he went out and wept bitterly" (Lk 22:62). St. Faustina tells how one day the Lord recalled her wretchedness to her and then looked on her with such affection that she thought she "would die for joy under that gaze."[15] Peter's story is in contrast with Judas'. By the time Judas betrayed Jesus, perhaps it had already been a long time since he had looked him in the eye. When, later, he regretted his act, he had neither the humility nor the courage to do so, though it might have saved him from despair.

"Learn from me; for I am gentle and lowly in heart, and you will find rest for your souls," Jesus tells us in Matthew 11:29. This is why his merciful love is a source of inner peace, and it's why we can say to him, "Most sacred and merciful heart of Jesus, grant us peace!" With the passing of time, the gospel teaching inspired the devotion to merciful love as a complement to the devotion to the Sacred Heart of Jesus. (The latter existed long before the private revelations of St. Margaret Mary of Alacoque, 1647–1690). Both devotions reflect the Church's progressive deepening (by divine aid) in the treasures of revelation. The devotion to the Divine Mercy originated in France, where it was conceived around the figure of St. Thérèse of Lisieux (1873–1897) and in Poland, where it was promoted by St. Faustina Kowalska (1905–1938). Prudence counsels caution about private revelations; they are not matters of Faith. Still, they merit our attention when they have been approved by Church authority.[16]

---

15. Kowalska, *Diary*, no. 881.

16. There are other books written by people to whom Christ has shown in a special manner his sorrowful and merciful heart. I do not cite them, because their authors are not canonized. See, for example, the work of the Servant of God Josefa Menéndez (1890–1923), a Spanish religious who died in France (*Un llamamiento al amor*, C. Cat. Salesiana, Madrid 1974); and the work of Gabrielle Bossis (1974–1950), a French playwright (*He and I*, Éditions Mediaspaul; 1st ed., January 1, 1985).

St. Faustina was canonized on April 30, 2000. That same day, Bl. John Paul II proclaimed that, in accordance with the desire expressed by Christ to St. Faustina, the Church would celebrate the Feast of Divine Mercy every second Sunday of Easter. As the saint herself wrote in her diary, the Lord wished that this feast "be a refuge and comfort for all souls and, especially for poor sinners. . . . The soul that will go to Confession and receive Holy Communion shall obtain forgiveness of sins and punishment."[17] This devotion focuses on trust in the divine goodness. St. Faustina says that Jesus told her, "Sins of distrust wound me most painfully."[18] For this reason, the saint advised repeating, "Jesus, I trust in you," which appears at the bottom of the painting that the Lord "commissioned," with two rays of light issuing from his heart.

St. Faustina's diary contains many urgent calls for the conversion of sinners. "Let the weak, sinful soul have no fear to approach Me, for even if it had more sins than there are grains of sand in the world, all would be drowned in the immeasurable depths of My mercy."[19] "The prayer most pleasing to Me," he told her on another occasion, "is prayer for the conversion of sinners. Know, My daughter, that this prayer is always heard and answered."[20] This insistence on praying for sinners is

---

17. Kowalska, *Diary*, no. 699. Sins involve both guilt and punishment. The sacrament of confession forgives the guilt. The punishment has to do with the sinner's purification and with justice (repair of harm done); in this twofold sense, penitence is a healing remedy on the way to healing the wounds of sin and, together with indulgences, a means of making up for "pending accounts." By way of example, if a thief apologizes for having robbed a certain amount of money, he can obtain forgiveness for his offense; still, on the one hand, since he has done damage to himself, he will have to make up for it with good works, and on the other, in strict justice, it is fitting to demand the restitution of the amount stolen, whether he himself pays (by doing penance) or another person does so in his place (indulgences).

18. Kowalska, *Diary*, no. 1976.

19. Kowalska, *Diary*, no. 1059.

20. Kowalska, *Diary*, no. 1397.

natural if we recall that eternal salvation is at stake, that recourse to the Divine Mercy is "the last hope of salvation,"[21] and that a sincere act of contrition would suffice to ensure that divine justice not have the last word. A twofold motive of love moves us to pray for those who don't yet trust Christ's mercy: empathy both with them and with the Lord's sorrows and joys. "Pray for souls," begs Jesus, "that they be not afraid to approach the tribunal of My mercy. Do not grow weary of praying for sinners. You know what a burden their souls are to My Heart. Relieve My deathly sorrow; dispense My mercy."[22]

St. Faustina's message insists on three points: spreading the devotion to the merciful love, praying for sinners, and being merciful to others. Bl. John Paul II points out in *Dives in misericordia* that one of the chief functions of the Church is to proclaim, practice, and beg for Divine Mercy. "Right from the beginning of my ministry," stated the Pope, ". . . I considered this message my special task. Providence has assigned it to me . . ."[23] In 2002, he consecrated the Sanctuary of Christ the Merciful in Lagiewniki, near Cracow, where St. Faustina died and is buried. It is striking that John Paul II died on the eve of a second Sunday of Easter, when the celebration of the Feast of Divine Mercy was being celebrated for the fifth time. As Stanislav Dziwisz recalls, the Holy Father died shortly after receiving Communion during Mass on this feast day.[24]

---

21. Kowalska, *Diary*, no. 1228.

22. Kowalska, *Diary*, no. 975.

23. John Paul II, Address of November 22, 1981, in Collevalenza, Italy.

24. "It was already almost eight o'clock," relates the Pope's secretary, "when suddenly I felt within a sort of categorical imperative: You must celebrate mass! And so I did. . . . It was the vigil mass of Divine Mercy Sunday, a solemnity so beloved of the Pope. . . . At Communion, I managed to give him, as viaticum, a few drops of the Most Precious Blood of Jesus Christ." S. Dziwisz, *Una vida con Karol* (Madrid: La Esfera de los Libros, 2007), p. 241.

JUSTICE AND MERCY

As St. Josemaría observes, Christ "subjected [himself] heroically to duty and acted with mercy."[25] The same love inspired the heroic sacrifice of the cross and his limitless mercy towards our wretchedness. If we imitate him, we will learn to combine a demanding and a compassionate approach towards ourselves and others. Holiness "is known by this double sign: heroic effort at absolute purity and limitless mercy for impurity."[26] These words of Gustave Thibon summarize Christian wisdom. These are two inseparable aspects of a single and unique love: generosity and humility, ascetic struggle and mercy, and exigency and compassion—towards ourselves and our fellow creatures.

It's not easy to reconcile these two aspects. The well-known Alcoholics Anonymous prayer reflects this: "Give me, Lord, the serenity to accept what I cannot change, the courage to change what I can, and the wisdom to know the difference." When faced with our own defects or someone else's, our motto might be: First (and always), compassion; second (sometimes, in what can be improved), exigency; and third, prudence to discern. Each element corrects the preceding one. It would be cold indifference and cowardice if we were "compassionate" toward others' defects but didn't help them to overcome them. Still, it is futile to correct people for things they cannot change: this would be tantamount to telling them we don't love them as they are.

Nor is there any contradiction between divine *justice* and *mercy*. Not only are they not opposed, each requires the other. St. Thérèse even affirms that when the day comes for her to

---

25. Escrivá, *Furrow*, no. 813.
26. Thibon, *L'echelle de Jacob* (Brussels: Éditions universitaires, 1945), p. 94.

stand before God, she will not take refuge in his mercy but in his justice, since he does not demand anything that surpasses the capacity of a weak little girl. She argues that "to be just means not only to exercise severity in punishing the guilty, but also to recognize right intentions and to reward virtue."[27]

In any case, it is no easy task to reconcile these two aspects when imparting Christian catechesis. The kindliness of God's mercy does not preclude the fact that his justice is demanding. Coming to know his merciful love is of great help to those with a tendency to scrupulosity, but it is well to recall his justice to those who think they can abuse divine goodness with impunity. If one explains the mysteries of the Faith with an excessive focus on personal responsibility before God's justice, one runs the risk of disfiguring his goodness and discouraging one's hearers. But it is equally true that to insist one-sidedly on mercy can foster irresponsibility and presumption. Thibon illustrated this difficult balance when she wrote, "I would like my thought to have power enough that it may not induce the just to sin, and tenderness enough that it may never bring sinners to despair; that I may neither present to the pure a less demanding God nor to the impure an inaccessible one."[28]

We've been focusing on God's mercy; it is only right that we indicate the implications of his justice as well. Perhaps people often misunderstand God and the afterlife because they are concentrating solely on how to enjoy their ephemeral days here on earth. But they are mistaken if they believe that heaven is assured to them if they simply take hold of

---

27. Thérèse of Lisieux, letter of May 9, 1897 to P. Roulland in *Divine Intimacy*, Vol. 3, by Gabriel of St. Mary Magdalen, no. 250 ("The Lord is Just") (San Francisco: Ignatius, 1987).

28. Thibon, *Nuestra mirada ciega*, p. 31.

God's goodness—proof that they have understood neither heaven nor real love. God wishes all to be saved (see 1 Tm 2:4) because he desires our good and yearns to be lovingly united with each of us, but this union requires that *we* love *him*. Heaven is the eternal consummation of a mutual love already present on earth. Only those who freely accept the divine invitation are admitted. Jesus made it very clear in his repeated calls to conversion: "Not every one who says to me, 'Lord, Lord,' shall enter the kingdom of heaven, but he who does the will of my Father who is in heaven" (Mt 7:21).

Those who naively think they have no need of conversion should be reminded how unjust it would be if God did not reward good actions, or if he let people commit evil ones with impunity. "*Charity*," observes Messori, "is not charity if it ignores or skips over the *truth*: the truth of our sin, whose present reality ought to have some weight if divine Justice is justice at all."[29] Trust in God without an effort to do what must be done to amend one's life is nothing new. The Old Testament addresses such presumption: "Do not say, 'His mercy is great, he will forgive the multitude of my sins,' for both mercy and wrath are with him, and his anger rests on sinners" (Sir 5:6). God is not mocked, although one need not foster a servile fear, either. As we have seen, we need only fear ourselves, since we may make evil use of our freedom. The saints teach us that the best fear is to detest sin because it saddens a Father who loves us immeasurably. Thus, when imparting catechesis, we would do well to rely on the same pedagogy God used to reveal himself progressively to human beings: first, the basic truths contained in the Old Covenant, then, to complete them, the full truth revealed by Christ and rooted in love.

---

29. V. Messori, *Hipótesis sobre María*, p. 350.

We have to dig deeply into the inexorable implications of justice in order to better understand the greatness of divine mercy. If we are honest, we are all aware of our moral responsibility. Perhaps only a person of delicate conscience perceives that he will have to render an account of the way he has used his money. On the other hand, it is easy to see the consequences of our free actions in extreme cases—all the more so if the responsible party is somebody else. Thus, when the police entrap a murderer, many people demand the full weight of justice. Accepting blame is easier when our decisions cause irreparable damage. If we steal money, we can make restitution, but if we murder someone, we can't bring the victim back to life, nor can we remedy the omission if we've withheld some aid that might have altered the life of somebody who has already died. We have to admit, in fact, the existence of a whole set of realities very closely linked together: freedom, responsibility, merit, blame, justice, judgment, recompense, and punishment. This is as natural as the law of gravity. No one is surprised that a stone falls to the ground by its own weight; the opposite would be unusual. Now let's apply this to the consequences of bad deeds. The firm purpose of amendment does not change the fact that the sin is indelible and irreversible, since it is in the past and can't be changed. This is on the *natural* level; the *supernatural* truth is that God, despite our guilt, gives us back our lost innocence. This is something as miraculous as a reversal of the law of gravity.

That God forgives us does not mean he doesn't take our sins seriously—in that case, injustice would remain. What actually happens is something more significant, and more unheard of. God does not look the other way before injustice, but he can do something immeasurably more beautiful than creating man from nothing. As Romano Guardini explains, divine pardon allows him to "recreate, to make new in all his original beauty the person tainted by guilt."[30] We stand before a great wonder:

> God places man, together with his sin, within himself, into a mystery of ineffable love. From there man emerges made new and innocent. God no longer has to turn his gaze away from this man, for his guilt no longer exists. Nor need our conscience turn from our person, for our guilt no longer exists.[31]

In fact, only someone who has glimpsed the depth of God's love can succeed in forgiving himself after a grave and irreparable act. It's difficult, for example, for a woman who repents of an abortion to reconcile with herself. Only a profoundly supernatural perspective could heal her distress.

The only remedy for merited punishment is clemency, which must be implored since it cannot be imposed. Coming before the tribunal of mercy, we acknowledge our guilt. Conscious of the impossibility of redoing our past, as a last resort, we turn to Jesus as advocate and beg pardon of his Father, appealing to his infinite mercy. These words of Guardini may inspire us to confess our sins:

> Lord, I accept your judgments. I stand before you and declare that I am the culprit. I want you to prevail in your judgment, for your will to prevail over my own, for I know that you are holy. I love you with all my being. You are in the right. With you, I will judge myself. But

---

30. Romano Guardini, *The Spirit of the Living God* (Barcelona: Belacqva, 2005), p. 67.
31. Guardini, *The Spirit of the Living God*, p. 65.

you are love, and I appeal to your love. With all that I am I surrender to your mystery of love. By no means do I claim the right to escape the rigor of your justice. But you are always grace.[32]

The result is astonishing: He forgives us and, moreover, we procure for him a joy in proportion to his love. St. Josemaría exclaims: "What depths of mercy there are in God's justice! For, in the judgments of men, he who confesses his fault is punished, and in the Judgment of God, he is pardoned. Blessed be the holy Sacrament of Penance!"[33]

WRETCHEDNESS AND GREATNESS

If we repent, ask God's forgiveness, and seek to amend our life, the reality of our wretchedness shifts to the background. The love of Christ assures us of a positive vision that translates into cultivating an attitude of humble self-esteem. The example of the saints illustrates this. "I am worth nothing," they often say. It doesn't disquiet them to see or acknowledge this, because they're aware of both their dignity as children of God and the benefits of their own weakness before a merciful lover. Their humility, in its perfect measure, is not like "the modesty of the one who does not think highly of himself and so remains in the background with a resigned attitude."[34] They have a realistic sense of their weakness, but thanks to the divine goodness, it doesn't trouble them. St. Josemaría, for example, saw himself before God . . .

---

32. Guardini, *The Spirit of the Living God*, pp. 67–68.
33. Escrivá, *The Way*, no. 309.
34. Von Hildebrand, *The Heart*, p. 169.

. . . as a poor street vendor, or like four bones with no physical strength, covered with scabs and wretchedness, a really ugly character. But, at the same time, what do I care, if I know that God loves me, that God's waiting for me, and that God can make use of me just as I am, and doesn't want to give me anything else on this earth! I'm happy, because this is how he likes me![35]

The saint knows how to "juggle" *wretchedness* and *greatness*. He sees his weakness but also how much the Lord loves him. "I am not a saint," said St. Thérèse; "I am a very little soul whom the good God has covered in graces . . ."[36] Awareness of being loved by God even entails a "holy pride," as if modesty would be out of place. "Perfect humility," observes C.S. Lewis, "dispenses with modesty. If God is satisfied with the work, the work may be satisfied with itself."[37] The consciousness of our limitations, as long as good will is not lacking, is no longer a crushing weight. Humility doesn't proceed from the rash presumption of thinking ourselves invulnerable, but from the maturity of living at peace with ourselves.

No one is so conscious of his or her littleness as the saints. This is not only because they notice their defects but above all because of the great contrast they perceive between their finite capacity to love and the unsearchable goodness of God. André Frossard recounts how, altogether undeservedly and unexpectedly, it was granted to him to contemplate the divine essence, as if he were the holiest of mystics. The result

35. In Echevarría, *Memoria del Beato Josemaría Escrivá*, 5th ed. (Madrid: Rialp, 2002), p. 81.

36. Thérèse of Lisieux, in M. van der Meersch, *Santa Teresita* (Madrid: Palabra, 1992), p. 140.

37. Lewis, *The Weight of Glory* (New York: HarperCollins, 1976), p. 38.

was a "dazzling consternation" upon realizing "the mud into which, all unknowing, I was sunk." His indignity was obvious before "the gentle violence of that light" that inundated him. The famous French journalist describes the "sort of overwhelming confusion" he experienced: "In my joy, I felt truly desolate to have nothing more to offer—in exchange for so much beauty—than an insignificant condensation of nothingness."[38] To explain why God doesn't manifest himself more frequently in this life, he says that the most impressive thing in him is not his omnipotence but his sweetness:

> What charity hides from our vision is the nuclear flash of the infinite which is contracted into an inconceivable humility. It is the eternal and pure innocence of God that breaks hearts. God cannot show himself without immediately moving us to judge ourselves and condemn ourselves without appeal or remission. And that's what God doesn't want. In him, all things spring from his love.[39]

The Lord, in his loving plan, illuminates things for us to the extent that we're able to process this explosive mixture of joy and confusion.

The saints are also especially aware of the dignity of being loved by God. Their holy pride can be the cause of perplexity if we confuse their strength of spirit with a hidden arrogance. But, as St. Paul indicates, their "competence is from God" (2 Cor 3:5). Aware of their weakness, they lean more on God and are able to take on the most daring initiatives. "I can do all things in him who strengthens me," said Paul in

---

38. A. Frossard, *No estamos solos. Mi experiencia de Dios* (Barcelona: Belacqva, 2005), p. 62.

39. Frossard, *No estamos solos*, pp. 64–65.

Philippians 4:13. The saints, in general, surprise us, having put on that "power . . . made perfect in weakness" (2 Cor 12:9). St. Josemaría expresses this idea, too:

> Our wisdom and our strength lie precisely in our being conscious of our littleness, of our nothingness in the eyes of God. But at the same time He himself is prompting us to get moving, to proclaim confidently his only begotten Son, Jesus Christ, even though we have errors and miseries, provided, that is, that as well as being weak, we are fighting to overcome our weakness.[40]

TAKING PRIDE IN ONE'S OWN FRAILTY

Having come this far, we might wonder: Are these reflections sufficient to reconcile us fully to ourselves? Yes and no. For some, they will be sufficient, but others—those especially afflicted with low self-esteem—will need to dig deeper into the effects of God's merciful love. What we've seen up to this point can help them to *accept themselves*, but it won't move them to *love themselves* enough that they wouldn't change places with anybody, even though they're acquainted with their own defects. Let's make a brief detour into the realm of mental health in order to understand the appropriateness of going further.

At a conference on neurotic disorders (depression, anxiety, insomnia, etc.) a prestigious psychiatrist underlined the usefulness of distinguishing three types of factors: *chemical variables* (symptoms due to a chemical imbalance), *precipitating variables* (such as stress due to conflict or frustration

---

40. Escrivá, *Friends of God*, no. 144.

induced by adversity), and *predisposing variables* (originating in the patient's personality, such as perfectionism or low self-esteem). The psychiatrist then presented the various treatment options. First, to address a chemical imbalance, there are medications (antidepressants, antianxiety drugs, and sleeping pills). Secondly, to address the circumstances that trigger the mental disorder, the doctor urges patients to relax, to detach from whatever is causing the stress, and to occupy themselves with other, more gratifying activities. But he didn't see any clear way to neutralize the root causes of these illnesses, the predisposing variables.

Someone in the audience asked the psychiatrist to go into more depth about how to help a patient overcome low self-esteem, recalling that this can be a root cause and therefore, until it was addressed, relapses in times of crisis would be inevitable. The specialist didn't know of any definitive solution. Regarding palliative remedies, he explained that he would ask the patient to fill out certain questionnaires so that he could analyze the negative features of his or her personality. Then, discussing the defects with the patient, he would limit himself to giving some practical advice (how to cultivate a more positive attitude and a sense of humor, or how to be more tolerant with oneself). Finally, he would try to encourage the patient, pointing out that we all have personal shortcomings, and that it's always possible to strengthen our positive traits to counteract the negative ones.

Much of what he said relates to our subject: A positive view of our flaws makes it so much easier for us to benefit from God's merciful love. We have said that we're like a car that needs gas to function: to preserve our mental health, we need to optimize our "mileage." People suffering from mental imbalances tend to have a tank that's both small and "leaky."

Therefore, in order to help them, medical remedies are insufficient. Merely prescribing drugs and counseling relaxation would be like pouring gasoline into a leaky tank.

If, seeking to encourage depressed people, we tell them only that everybody has defects, they may end up accepting this but still wish they could exchange their own flaws for a different set. This doesn't solve the problem. If they don't accept themselves as they are, they will be unlikely ever to enjoy inner peace. Sándor Márai recreates this situation in a novel in which two old people are reminiscing about their life. One says to the other:

> In the depths of your soul there's a convulsive feeling, a constant wish, a wish to be different from the way you are. It's the greatest misfortune destiny can punish a person with. . . . We have to adjust to what we are . . . to know and accept that we're vain, egotistical, bald, and pot-bellied.[41]

To some degree, we must all solve the same basic problem. Our self-esteem won't be sufficiently stable until we discover the true reasons for being content with ourselves as we are. If we know that the Lord loves us *despite* our defects, we won't yet have sounded the depths of his merciful love. *Love of oneself* is much more than *self-acceptance*. People with low self-esteem whose relatives recall frequently how much they love them may be comforted—but not cured. As long as they believe they're worthless people with an indulgent family, the root problem will never be resolved. This will only happen when they discover that the love they receive is not due only to the benevolence of others but also to a certain loveableness in themselves.

---

41. Sándor Márai, *El último encuentro* (Barcelona: Emecé, 1999), p. 120.

There is something of *egotism* in needing to be loved not only because of the lover's goodness but also for one's own value. It's a universal law. We would be insulted if someone called us unbearable but assured us that he was willing to overlook our flaws out of kindness. The more perfect the love we receive, the more we're loved as we really are. God is the one who goes furthest of all. Only he is altogether capable of loving us—not only *despite* our flaws but *because of* them, and even *thanks to* them. We know from experience that human love is not as disinterested. We manage, perhaps, to love certain defects so that the depth of our love for another increases. There is something divine, for instance, in the love of a mother who appears delighted to adopt a child with no arms. There are some defects that awaken love. It is easy to feel compassion for someone we see weeping, or for children who don't conceal their neediness. But it is very difficult to continually love a repulsive defect, such as ill-temper or rudeness.

What else, besides our debility, could serve as foundation for this healthy pride? We all possess *some* good qualities, but they aren't sufficient to guarantee our self-esteem. Our pride will remain unsatisfied until we learn to love our shortcomings as well. And we'll only be able to do this if they prevent some advantage when it comes to the person we most want to love us. To the extent that we establish a mutual relationship of love with Christ, his "weak spot" for our littleness helps us to be reconciled to it, too. If we live for his esteem, we'll love ourselves *with* our defects and, in a certain sense, *with gratitude* for them. What most attract his merciful love are the needs that he can relieve. Thus, if we're in harmony with his sorrowful and compassionate heart, we'll be aware of the consolation he feels each time we ask forgiveness, and we'll share in the joy we procure for him. This *humble pride in our weakness* doesn't entail loving the weakness as such. One accepts it gladly because it offers a chance to gladden the Lord's heart. Humble self-esteem is the best antidote against problems of pride.

A few examples can serve to illustrate the Christian's joy upon perceiving Christ's predilection for the very weakest. We stand before him like a poor stockholder who owns a single share of a major company but feels confident of his clout in negotiations with a magnate who lacks only that share for an absolute majority. Or we're like the owner of an object of very little value, such as an ancient, broken-down chair, for which a millionaire antique collector is ready to pay an enormous sum. This is the way all our flaws are "reevaluated" with Christ.

Opening the Gospels to any page at all proves Christ's predilection for the poor (in the biblical sense, "poor" means one who lacks something.) He tells us he has not come for the righteous but for sinners, that there is greater joy in heaven for one sinner who converts than for ninety-nine righteous people, that the Good Shepherd goes in search of the lost sheep. . . . From the saints—Mary, above all— we learn to live by this new logic. In the Magnificat, she attributes all her divine privileges to her lowliness (see Lk 1:48). St. Paul, too, wonders at this evangelical logic when he declares that he glories in his weaknesses (see 2 Cor 12:9–10). Without a doubt, St. Thérèse is the one who has pointed most clearly to this healthy pride. Paraphrasing our Mother's hymn of praise, she says: "The Almighty has done great things for me, and the greatest is to show me my littleness and my helplessness for any good."[42] Finally, St. Faustina tells us, "As the soul continues to immerse itself more deeply into

---

42. Thérèse of Lisieux, in *The Message of St. Thérèse of Lisieux* (San Francisco: Ignatius Press, 1997), p. 15.

the abyss of its nothingness and need, God uses his omnipotence to exalt it."[43]

The logic of mercy experienced by the saints helps us to approach the struggle for sanctity realistically. Leaving behind our daydreams of impossible gestures, adventures, and sacrifices, we center on the little things of every day. The realism of humility counteracts the fantasies of vanity. As St. Thérèse writes in a letter:

> I have seen by experience, when I feel nothing, when I am incapable of praying and practicing any virtue, that this is the time to seek little opportunities, little nothings which please Jesus more than the dominion of the whole world and even more than martyrdom borne generously. For example, a smile, a kindly word, when I feel like keeping silent or showing an annoyed expression, and so on. Do you understand? It isn't to work on my crown, to gain merits: it's to please Jesus . . ."[44]

The new evangelical logic gives rise to happy paradoxes, like the joy that many old and sick people experience upon discovering that the less they're worth in the eyes of others, the more valuable they are in the eyes of God. Something similar happens with the interior struggle if we're "in sync" with the Lord. Being motivated by love for him and for others inspires us to strive to improve. Still, face-to-face with him, in a certain sense we no longer care whether we achieve this or not, since we please him equally by preparing gifts for him or allowing him to give them to us. St. Thérèse even said that if there were nothing to offend the Lord in her falls, she would

---

43. Kowalska, *Diary*, no. 593.
44. Thérèse of Lisieux, quoted in Manglano, *Orar con Teresa de Lisieux*, p. 61.

fall just to give him the joy of helping her to rise again. We can apply this to any aspect of our daily struggle. For example, the effort to smile in adversity: If we make our final accounting at day's end and find that we have conquered only two times out of ten, we can first offer the Lord these two victories and then allow him to love us in our eight defeats. In this mutual relation of love, both he and we can end the day with two joys, plus eight more. Thus, if our ultimate life's goal is really to please the Lord, our main objective is already assured. The more we struggle, the better: the more chances we will have to give him joy.

These happy paradoxes are countless. I'll add just one more: what makes God most inclined to concede his graces is our littleness, humbly acknowledged. St. Vincent de Paul explains it:

> Only when we renounce self-seeking completely, when we fling ourselves, truly convinced of our nothingness, upon God's heart, and when we abandon ourselves without reserve to his will, only then will we see that the Lord has long been standing at our door, to bring us his peace, his light, his consolations.[45]

We've already mentioned the sonnet in which Lupe de Vega wonders why the Lord loves us so much. It begins: "What interest pursues you, my Jesus?" Certainly, all the Lord's "interest" is in the opportunities to love us that our weaknesses offer him. The less we seek to shine, the more he can. That Castillian poet said in his prayer: "Lord forgive what I am for the sake of what I love." Paraphrasing, each of us

---

45. In W. Hünermann, *El Padre de los pobres. Vida de San Vincente de Paúl* (Madrid: Palabra, 1995), p. 209.

can add, "If I don't know how to love you, then you love me; forgive what I am for the sake of the way I let myself be loved."

Two Conditions

There are two conditions without which pride in one's own weakness isn't possible: *good will* and *mutual love*. If we didn't battle our defects, our love would not be sincere or genuine. And what use would it be for Christ to love us with our defects if we didn't love him? He forgives us when we sincerely ask for forgiveness, but he doesn't deny our guilt. We've already seen that his mercy is not compatible with the presumption that encourages repeated sin. Nor is that mercy compatible with a harsh exigency that takes no notice of what is possible or impossible for the sinner. The incident of the woman taken in adultery is very eloquent in this regard: The Lord pardons her gladly but instructs her not to sin again (see Jn 8:1–11).

Let's begin with the first condition: the good will to combat our defects. One might erroneously think that if the Lord is so delighted to forgive us, he doesn't care whether we sin or not. St. Thérèse worried that her teachings on merciful love might serve as an excuse for "spiritual quietism." She told one companion, "Our little way, wrongly understood, could be mistaken for quietism or illuminism. . . . Do not think that to live our little way is to follow a path of relaxation, full of sweetness and consolation. Just the opposite!"[46] This saint's example provides a decisive counterbalance to the lingering influence of Jansenism, a heresy that focused excessively on the rigorous fulfillment of moral duty. This was

---

46. In M.-D. Poinsenet, *Thérèse de Lisieux*, p. 362.

nothing new—the same confusion already existed in the days of St. Paul, when Christ's message was a great novelty for the Pharisaic mentality. In this context, the Apostle affirms that it is not works that save, but faith, indicating that trust in the love of God revealed in Christ is more important than the minute fulfillment of the Mosaic law. Then, to clarify that he was not claiming to abolish the moral law, he asked, "What then? Are we to sin because we are not under law but under grace? By no means!" (Rom 6:15). Here St. Paul is protecting us against the pride that hides behind moralism. To ensure the rectitude of intention in our aspirations to holiness, he recommends that we trust more in God's love than in our own merits. As St. Thérèse cries, "One must fight! Fight to the end! Even with no hope of victory. Even in total defeat. To the death! Combat without ceasefire! Even with no hope of winning the battle. What does success matter?"[47]

Merciful love mitigates the pride that demands victories, but we wouldn't truly love the Lord if we didn't make an effort to offer him happiness through our little everyday victories. Without this effort at progress, we would be abusing his kindness. Christ loves everything about us except our ill will (or our lack of good will)—unless we acknowledge it and, asking forgiveness, recover our happiness. Pride diminishes, but the love that urges us on remains intact: not only our concern to avoid wounding the heart of Jesus with our lukewarmness, but also because, as we saw when addressing coredemption, we perceive his sorrow at the many sins committed daily.

As for the second condition, humble pride in one's own littleness is not viable if there's no love for Christ in us. If we're indifferent to him, that humble esteem is impossible.

---

47. Thérèse of Lisieux, in Van der Meersch, *Santa Teresita*, p. 133.

Our shortcomings will indeed cease to upset us once we discover the advantages of bringing them before a merciful lover, but in order to accept gladly something negative, we must love the one who loves us. It's not that he *likes* weakness as such: he *loves* it because he feels our joy as his own and knows the happiness we feel every time he forgives us and helps us. From our point of view, as long as we fail to "connect with" his grateful heart, we won't experience the consolation that comes of discovering his "soft spot" for our neediness.

To illustrate the importance of this mutual love, imagine that we have a complex because of some defect that has tormented us since childhood: the size of our ears, or shyness about public speaking, for example. The complex may have snowballed to the point of becoming a serious obstacle to our relationships. It may not ever disappear entirely, but it will at least be neutralized when someone loves us and we realize that we have given the defect an exaggerated importance. If a mutual love relationship is established, it may even happen that the objectively negative trait amounts to something positive. Love doesn't alter the reality, but what was an insurmountable and embarrassing obstacle becomes a cause for joy. Each of us could place before God a whole series of shortcomings that give us complexes: weaknesses, imperfections, limitations, wounds from the past, ineptitude, incompetence, wretchedness, littleness. . . . A sincere examination of conscience suffices to detect this whole gloomy background— which is then transformed into the focus of joy, thanks to God's love.

If we're in tune with his sorrowful and grateful heart, we'll rejoice at victories and defeats alike. If we rejoice only when we attain our goals, it's a sign that we lack rectitude of intention. It makes sense that our successes should be gratifying, but there are two possible reasons for this: one good (the joy we give the Lord) and one bad (our vanity). If our failures sadden us, this means that he is not our main motive for success. At bottom, it is the same love of God that leads us to offer him generous sacrifices or allow ourselves to be loved when we fail. Pride inspires our efforts if we make an effort to give him joy but don't accept his love. And if we never try to surprise him with gifts, we don't truly love him either—in which case we won't be able to rejoice at receiving gifts from him. We might compare this to an *embrace*. *Embracing* and *being embraced* unite in a single gesture. It's not possible to embrace someone who's not willing to be embraced. It's a reciprocal gesture, no matter which of the two takes the initiative of surrender, for here *to receive* is already *to give*. The same thing happens in love for Christ. We allow ourselves to be embraced when he forgives us or helps us, and we embrace him each time we offer him something. The joy, in both cases, is mutual.

In light of this, we can more deeply understand the difference between *perfect* and *imperfect contrition*. With perfect contrition, we suffer with the pain of Christ's heart at our sins, and we also share his joy once we've been pardoned. With imperfect contrition, sadness prevails: We ask forgiveness, but our pride prevents us from forgiving ourselves. Egotistical self-love wants nothing but victories. But the Lord is easier to please than our pride; he only expects us to allow ourselves to be loved, and to show our love by a sincere effort to increase in virtue.

SPIRITUAL CHILDHOOD

"Little" St. Thérèse—as she herself, before her death, asked to be invoked—left us a way of relating to the Lord that she called the way of spiritual childhood. The teaching of this doctor of the Church meant a great advance in Christian spirituality. In classical manuals on humility, it was said that our miseries help us to make spiritual progress because they bring us to realize the need to be forgiven by a God who loves us despite our defects.[48] However, from the time of St. Thérèse onward, a new nuance was introduced: God loves us not only *despite* but, in a certain way, also *because of* our weakness. The Lord is very generous and wishes to "bend over backwards" for everyone, but he has a "soft spot" for the weakest of all, since if they persevere in their efforts and acknowledge their weakness, he can truly overturn things for them.

St. Paul intuited the same thing when the Lord told him, "My power is made perfect in weakness"—and, the Apostle added, "I will all the more gladly boast of my weaknesses, that the power of Christ may rest upon me. For the sake of Christ, then, I am content with weaknesses. . . ." (2 Cor 12:9–10). St. Josemaría affirms:

> As we sense in our hearts the love, the compassion, the tenderness of Christ's gaze upon us, for he never abandons us, we shall come to understand the full meaning of those words of St. Paul, *virtus in infirmitate perficitur.* If we have faith in Our Lord, in spite of our failings, or, rather, with our failings—we shall be faithful to our Father, God . . .[49]

Thus, we too can attain sanctity, not only *despite* our miseries but *with* them. Thanks to them, we will love God even more.

---

48. See, for instance, the classic book by Joseph Tissot, *How to Profit from Your Faults* (New Rochelle: Scepter Publishers, 2004), written in the mid-nineteenth century, which collects the teachings of St. Francis de Sales.

49. Escrivá, *Friends of God*, no. 194.

We do well, then, to be like little children who aren't shocked at their own weakness. God helps us to conduct ourselves with fortitude as long as we remain in this frailty that attracts his gifts. The "little one" is the one to whom he can always give something. It's the "adult" who begins to think he can manage things by himself. He's lost—at least, in terms of sanctity. Thérèse demonstrated with her life that her "little way" is very much a shortcut to this noble goal. She tells us that she had a very insecure personality, but when she discovered the great advantage of her debility, everything began to run smoothly—her spirit, finally freed from scrupulosity, expanded.

Spiritual childhood colors the relationship with our Father God; it leads us to imitate the simple prayer of children, the limitless confidence they have in their parents, their spontaneity and naughty tricks. As St. Thérèse insists, "To be little . . . is to not be discouraged by one's own failings. Little children *fall frequently*. But they're too little to hurt themselves when they do."[50] We can learn a lot from observing children. They have, for instance, a particular sense of justice. Accustomed as they are to receiving everything for free, when their father gives them some candies, they take one and give it away in a show of generosity. They get into mischief, too, but they know how to get to the heart of things. I once heard a child say, "I asked Jesus to forgive me because sometimes I stop loving him."

The behavior of children when they're asking for forgiveness is especially edifying. St. Thérèse recalled one such scene:

> Imagine a child who has just displeased his mother with
> a temper tantrum or some disobedience. If he runs to a

---

50. Thérèse of Lisieux, quoted in Van der Meersch, *Santa Teresita*, pp. 134–135.

corner to sulk and screams for fear of punishment, his
mother will surely not be moved to forgive him, but if
he puts his arms around her, smiling and saying to her,
"Give me a kiss; I won't do it again," will not the mother
tenderly hold him to her heart and forget his childish mischief . . . ? Even so, she knows very well that her little
one will be up to his old tricks at the next opportunity—
but it doesn't matter: if he wins her heart again, he'll never
be punished.[51]

St. Josemaría describes spiritual childhood as well,[52] and
this has made it accessible to ordinary Christians who are
unfamiliar with a convent atmosphere. Spiritual childhood
is adaptable to any mentality, and it is at once tender and
firm. Some of his descriptions are especially memorable, like
this one:

We've got to be convinced that God is always near us. We
live as though he were far away, in the heavens high above,
and we forget that he is also continually by our side.

He is there like a loving father. He loves each one of
us more than all the mothers in the world can love their
children—helping us, inspiring us, blessing . . . and
forgiving.

How often have we misbehaved and then cleared
the frowns from our parents' brows, telling them: I
won't do it anymore!—The same day, perhaps, we fall
again . . . and our father, with feigned harshness in his
voice and serious face, reprimands us, while in his heart

51. Manglano, *Orar con Teresa de Lisieux*, p. 14.
52. See especially *The Way*, nos. 864, 882, 887, 894, and 896 and *Forge*, nos.
345–347.

he is moved, realizing our weakness and thinking: poor child, how hard he tries to behave well!

We've got to be filled, to be imbued with the idea, that our Father, and very much our Father, is God who is both near us and in heaven.[53]

The way of childhood immunizes us against a voluntaristic mindset. It helps us to understand that holiness consists of a perfection of love, not in titanic efforts to compensate for whatever negative view we may have of ourselves. In his prayer, St. Josemaría would even say, "Jesus, I could never repay you, even if I died of Love, for the grace you have spent on me in making me little."[54] It's not a question of letting up in the struggle. St. Thérèse recounts that ever since she was three years old, she couldn't remember ever having denied God anything. But knowing herself to be a little, favorite daughter helped her to purify the intention that inspired her spiritual struggle. She writes in one of her letters: "Jesus teaches me not to count up my acts. He teaches me to do all things through love. . . . But this is done in peace, in abandonment."[55]

Becoming like little children means first of all abandoning ourselves into the hands of God. This "abandonment" means primarily a *loving surrender*: allowing ourselves to be loved, putting our entire life into God's hands, letting him do what he wants with us. Being like children also requires *faith* and *humility*. To trust in God means not worrying about the future—having total confidence in his omnipotent and loving providence. We leave our own value and esteem in his hands.

53. Escrivá, *The Way*, no. 267.

54. No. 901. Note the double meaning of "little."

55. In M.-D. Poinsenet, *Thérèse de Lisieux, Témoin de la Foi* (Paris: Collection Super/Editions G. P, 1962), p. 323.

Some fail to see the attraction of spiritual childhood, thinking it "puerile or childish."[56] They don't understand that "all this is not utter nonsense, but a sturdy and solid Christian life."[57] It makes others uncomfortable: it's difficult for them to admit how much they need it. Although one can't force this on others, it's good to make clear that the Holy Spirit shows all prayerful souls the wonder of this way of spiritual childhood sooner or later.

Since the realization of God's love doesn't eliminate pride entirely, spiritual childhood is the best way to neutralize it. We need to be on guard: sometimes *amor propio* (love of self) rules us imperceptibly. This happens when instead of leaning on the Lord like children conscious of their littleness, we begin to trust in our own strength as self-sufficient "grown-ups." It's clear: We spend our whole life playing the role of the prodigal son. Becoming like little children makes it easier to live in a permanent state of conversion. As Bl. John Paul II teaches, the authentic knowledge of God is a "constant and inexhaustible source of conversion, not only as a momentary interior act but also as a permanent attitude, as a state of mind. Those who come to know God in this way, who 'see' him in this way, can live only in a state of being continually converted to him."[58]

Perhaps God doesn't free us from pride once and for all so that we can continue to be little children. It almost seems as if the Redemption were incomplete. St. Paul came to this conclusion:

---

56. *The Way*, no. 854.
57. *The Way*, no. 853.
58. John Paul II, *Dives in misericordia*, no. 13.

And to keep me from being too elated by the abundance of revelation, a thorn was given me in the flesh, a messenger of Satan, to harass me, to keep me from being too elated. Three times I besought the Lord about this, that it should leave me, but he said to me, "My grace is sufficient for you, for my power is made perfect in weakness." I will all the more gladly boast of my weaknesses, that the power of Christ may rest on me. For the sake of Christ, then, I am content with weakness (2 Cor 12:7–10).

In some way, it is good for us that our pride does not vanish altogether: it gives us abundant material for interior struggle and serves to alert us when we distance ourselves from God. To the extent that we cease to be like children and begin taking ourselves too seriously, pride makes us feel uncomfortable. Close to the Lord, we breathe "pure air." As soon as we start to leave him, the "air" begins to get "rarified" and "strained." Thanks to how uncomfortable we feel each time we fall and turn our backs on him, we feel the need to take refuge in his merciful arms, return to intimacy with him, and be filled with joy.

From children we learn, finally, not to give ourselves airs. Merciful love allows us to live on earth the same humility that is enjoyed in heaven.

Epilogue

It is natural to end this book on a note of hope: We've addressed all sorts of problems, but the answer to them is the love of God. An abundance of shared experiences over the last twenty years permits me to foresee excellent prospects for those who fully abandon themselves to the love Christ has revealed to us. In cataloguing the abundant fruits of the awareness and lived experience of this love, I have been especially struck by the decisive turn the lives of certain people have taken. Some have even been able to stop taking medications they had needed for years. However, the most common result is a more or less dramatic increase in the depth, or quality, of their love upon *improving their attitude towards themselves and others.*

Indeed, God's love makes the injustice of pride obvious. We grow vividly aware that we no longer need to act out of vanity. We endeavor to become better, but we see the absurdity of doing so to make ourselves worthy, or to merely feel good about ourselves. Our motives for keeping up the struggle grow more disinterested, and we discover a great interior freedom. Knowing that we are loved so much purifies our heart. Possessiveness vanishes, and we lose our fear of loving others. The affection we receive in return is gratifying, but we no longer crave it. *Detachment* finally becomes possible.

Before, the only way to avoid the urge to possess the beloved was to love less. Now, it's possible to love more, and well. This is a great discovery for all those who have long debated how to reconcile apparent contradictions between affection and detachment, dependence and independence, fortitude and sensitivity.

A lively sense of God's love transforms our attitude towards him. The conscience is no longer rigid; the scruples that have caused so much suffering fade away. Pious practices are no longer motivated by the fear of "getting in trouble" with God. Our relationship with him is now entirely different. It becomes possible to enjoy a close and mutual friendship that is ever deepening, but we also have at our disposal something that captivates him: our deficiencies. For someone in love, just allowing oneself to be loved makes one very happy. This can be the daily battle of one who is in sync with the compassionate and sorrowful heart of Christ: that every humiliation recall his merciful glance; that every pain enkindle the wish to be in harmony with him, easing the wounds of his heart; that every case of wounded pride leads us to return like a prodigal son; and that every wounded heart be an occasion of coredeeming with him. This "bill of exchange" allows every trouble we offer him to be transformed into a reason for joy.

Thanks to God's merciful love, humiliations are now ruled out. Perhaps they're still possible objectively, but not subjectively: Nothing and no one can humiliate those who know themselves to be children of God. While an insecure person might get upset at the slightest provocation, someone who depends solely on God's "opinion" might suffer from a wounded heart but not from wounded pride. Once we exchange "human respect" for "divine respect," all that matters is whether others allow themselves to be loved.

Thus, we cultivate that humble self-esteem that guarantees an unshakeable inner peace. We live at peace with ourselves, with God, and with other people. We get the impression that life and its constant hustle and bustle are slowed down, as if we were driving downhill and a touch of the brakes now and then is sufficient. We're carefree, like a three- or four-year-old child—except that a child grows up and begins to be aware of its deficiencies, and then the trouble begins.

If happiness consists of peace and joy, we're already halfway there. The second part—the joy—will keep increasing indefinitely to the extent that we contribute to the happiness of the Lord and of others. We need to struggle without ceasing, but it's all a prelude to heavenly beatitude.

I conclude by translating from the French something sent to me by a friend called "Love Me Just As You Are!" The author emphasizes the excellence of God's love and the significance of our response, poor as it may be. These reflections may help us put the finishing touches on all we have covered.

> I know your wretchedness, the struggles and tribulations of your soul and the weakness of your sickly body; I know your cowardice, your sins, your dejection, and yet I tell you "Give me your heart, love me just as you are!" If you wait to be an angel before abandoning yourself and giving yourself to Love, you'll never love me. Although you fall over and over into those faults that you would never wish to commit, although you may be so weak in the practice of virtue: I will bear everything, except your refusal to love me. At every instant and in every state of mind in which you may find yourself, in fervor as in dryness, love me just as you are! I want the love of your needy heart; if

you wait to be perfect to love me, you'll never love me. Am I not able to make of every grain of sand a seraph, radiant in purity, nobility, and love? Could I not, with a single movement of my will, make thousands of saints arise out of nothingness, a thousand times more perfect and loveable than the ones I have created? Am I not the *Omnipotent One*? And if I have wished to leave unmade forever all these marvelous beings, and have preferred your poor love to theirs?

My child, let me love you. Give me your heart. I surely mean to help you to grow better, but meanwhile, I love you as you are. In you, I love even your fragility. The love of the poor pleases me: I wish that from their indigence this cry might arise continually: "Lord, I love you." What do I want with your knowledge and your talents? I could have destined you for great matters, but no, you will be the unprofitable servant. I only ask that you love! Love will bring you to do all the rest without your realizing it; only try to fill the present moment with love; try to fulfill each of your little duties out of love.

Today, I come like a beggar to the door of your heart, I, the Lord of Lords. I knock and I wait: open quickly; don't tell me you are wretched, don't tell me you are not worthy. If you knew all your neediness, you would have died of pain. The only thing that could wound my heart would be to see you doubt or lack trust in me. I will give you a love much more perfect than you ever dreamed. But remember this: *love me just as you are!*

Let us not forget to turn to the Virgin Mary. After a sin, pride may cause us to lose sight of the Lord's merciful face.

But we can always dare to go to our mother: She always smiles upon us, and, as Pope Benedict XVI affirms, "This smile, a true reflection of God's tenderness, is the source of an invincible hope."[1] After the heart of Jesus, the heart of Mary is the most faithful reflection of divine love. In her, how close we come to the maternally merciful face of God the Father!

---

1. Benedict XVI, Homily of September 15, 2008.